LEARNING THROUGH PLAY

HARPER & ROW, Publishers   New York, Evanston, San Francisco, London

LEARNING THROUGH PLAY

by

JEAN MARZOLLO and JANICE LLOYD

Illustrated by IRENE TRIVAS

Grateful acknowledgment is made for permission to reprint the
following:

"The Bus Song," page 16. Adapted and arranged with new lyrics
by Tom Glazer; copyright 1960, Songs Music, Inc., Scarborough,
N.Y. By permission.

The alphabet chart on page 55, provided through the courtesy of
Palmer Method Handwriting, Schaumburg, Illinois.

FIRST EDITION

STANDARD BOOK NUMBER: 06-012819-4

LIBRARY OF CONGRESS CATALOG CARD NUMBER: 78-144182

To
Claudio
and
Juliette

To
Richard

To

Allonia Gadsden

and

Beth Kolehmainen

for their perceptive insights
and creative suggestions

CONTENTS

Introduction

This is a book for parents of preschoolers. It is for mothers and fathers who enjoy their children and marvel at the ways they grow—physically, emotionally and intellectually. It is for loving parents who know that the best gifts they can give to their children are the gifts of affection, attentiveness and respect. The emphasis of the book is on learning, in particular, on helping preschoolers learn at home. It is written for parents, because they, more than anyone else, are closest to a child in his early years and most able to assist the development of his full potential.

Important discoveries about the nature of early childhood have occurred in the last decade—discoveries that reveal how much a child can, wants and *needs* to learn before he enters first grade. Such discoveries have been passed on to teachers but, except for rare instances, not to the people who have the most interest of all, parents. Our hope is that this book will provide insights about early education and a wealth of interesting activities for parents to share with their children.

A Changing Concept of Early Childhood We used to assume that the first six years of a child's life was a time for fun and physical growth. We preferred not to "educate" a child until he was of school age. "Let the kid alone. He'll never have it so good again for the rest of his life" was a familiar refrain that typified yesterday's philosophy of early childhood.

We weren't completely wrong. Play *is* the most important aspect of a young child's life. But we weren't completely right either. We thought that play and education were opposite things. Now we know better. In the last decade, educational experts and early-childhood specialists have discovered that play *is* learning, and even more, that play is one of the *most effective* kinds of learning known.

Another way to say this is that the young child is one of the best learners we know. During his preschool years a child learns more—faster—than at any other time in his life. Some learning psychologists have estimated that *by the age of five*, a child's intelligence quotient (IQ) is basically established. They say that by this age attitudes toward learning and patterns of thinking have settled into one's mind, and that these same attitudes and patterns guide a person's thoughts for the rest of his life. What does this mean?

It means that the concept of early childhood as merely a time for fun and physical growth is outdated and inadequate. We now know that the early-childhood years are exciting and powerful years for building the foundations of human intelligence. We see the act of play as the extraordinary educational process by which it happens.

The Power of Play Play is the natural way a child learns. It is the way he learns to concentrate, to exercise his imagination, to try out ideas, to practice grown-up behavior, to develop a sense of control over his world.

We expect that if you take the time to look for the instructional value of your child's play, you'll be amazed, as others have been, at the fervent intensity that children bring to play activities. It is as if they are little researchers, working at a job that they love. Young children at play combine a seriousness of purpose with an enjoyment that adults often envy.

Nature has always been on the side of early learning. When children are born, they are graced with an insatiable sense of curiosity. They want to touch, smell, taste, see and hear everything. The more they learn, the more they want to learn. They want to talk, they want to imitate other people, they want to explore.

Because of this strong urge, young children are exceptionally open to environmental influences. In a home where discovery is discouraged, children often learn how *not* to learn, a tragic outcome, to say the least. In homes where early explorations are encouraged, the minds and personalities of children grow and develop the potential that is each child's natural legacy.

Someday, maybe, there will exist a well-informed, well-considered and yet fervent public conviction that the most deadly of all possible sins is the mutilation of a child's spirit.
—Erik Erikson, Harvard University

A child's spirit is that unique combination of curiosity and pleasure with which he seeks to learn. This spirit can be weakened or strengthened depending on outside influences. The purpose of this book is to provide a ready reference for parents who want to be sure that a sense of excitement and a love of learning is fostered in their homes.

The Parents' Role   In brief, the parents' responsibilities for the early education of their child are:

—to understand the skills their child needs to learn,
—to introduce activities and materials that lead to learning,
—to take an interest in learning discoveries,
—to interpret and enlarge experiences,
—to relate learning to the child's overall framework of knowledge
—to have patience with weaknesses and praise for strengths

Parents also have a responsibility to keep "education" in proper perspective. Sometimes overzealous mothers, with Harvard in mind, try to rush the process of learning. They think that the faster a child learns, the more he learns. Not true. Overzealous mothers often discover, much to their dismay, that the main lesson their child learns is that learning is no fun at all. As Samuel Johnson once said, "You teach your daughters the diameters of the planets and wonder what you have done that they do not delight in your company."

The best and most effective kind of parent is the one who accepts his child for what he is and encourages him to develop his potential at his own rate. This parent isn't frantic about education, rather, he enjoys a child's learning discoveries as one exciting aspect of overall growth. Sharing but never forcing the natural development of his child, this parent seems to sense what good teachers know:

Children learn from experiences that are concrete and active   For a child to understand the abstract concept of "roundness," he must first have many experiences with real round things. He needs time to feel round shapes, to roll around balls, to think

4

about the similarities between round objects and to look at pictures of round things. When children are at play, they like to push, pull, poke, hammer and otherwise manipulate objects, be they toy trucks, egg cartons or pebbles. It is this combination of action and concreteness that makes play so effective as an educational process.

Children are always ready to learn on their own level   They are ready both in terms of ability and desire. Part of sharing intellectual growth with a child is identifying what he knows and what he doesn't know. The best parents and teachers seem to be able to sense appropriate activities that provide the right amount of interest and challenge for a child without being too difficult. They know that success promotes learning.

Children have individual learning styles   What works for one child may not work for another. Skills that come easily to one child may be difficult for another and vice versa. It is important for parents to sense differences and to avoid comparing children in any way that may make one feel inferior.

Children learn a language from hearing it and trying it themselves   Many parents talk to their children from the time they are born. And without a doubt, the children who grow up in these rich verbal environments tend to be very adept with language.

Nevertheless, we want to suggest that talking with a child is a technique that can be overdone. Some well-meaning parents rob their child of his peace by bombarding him constantly with verbal information. Too much of a good thing won't work. It is best to talk naturally and casually with your child so that he will learn language skills readily but unself-consciously.

FURTHERMORE

Providing effective learning experiences   This is something of an art. It seems to be a matter of suggesting the right activity at the right time. There's a knack to it that involves, first of all, being familiar enough with preschool skills so that you can shape a play experience with objectives in mind; second, recognizing what it is that your child is discovering; and third, using what is available to enlarge and expand the discovery for him. If the process seems complicated, don't be overly concerned. This book has been designed especially to help you set the stage for learning and relate an experience to the overall intellectual framework that is slowly being constructed in your child's mind.

As you use this book, you'll probably invent new learning games of your own. If so, the book will have been a success. We could never have listed all the experiences through which children learn—for they are infinite. What we tried to do realistically was to select enough activities to cover the important preschool skills. We tried to give a sense of the many ways to teach them. Eventually, we hope these techniques will come naturally to you and that you will use this book only as a reminder of activities that have slipped your mind.

Eleven Skill-Families The learning experiences in this book have been organized into eleven chapters, each of which focuses on a particular group of skills. The reason for this is simply to achieve a clarity of explanation. In reality, children do not learn compartmentally. That is, they do not learn counting skills one day and language skills the next. Rather, their education is much more organic. Given the right kind of learning atmosphere, mental ability grows naturally and experientially. Initially inspired by inner motivations, a child's learning process thrives on encouragement, challenge and a sense of pleasure.

In order for parents and teachers to provide help, they must understand the kinds of learning that a child experiences. It may be helpful to think of the chapters of this book as representing different skill-families.

These families are:

1. The Five Senses
2. Language Development
3. Prereading
4. Understanding Relationships
5. Sorting and Classifying
6. Counting and Measuring
7. Problem Solving
8. Exploring
9. Creativity
10. Self-Esteem
11. Physical Growth

Each chapter begins with a discussion of a particular skill-family and an activity chart that defines the objectives of each play experience. For optimum effectiveness, we suggest that you read the introductory material before you select an activity. In this way, you will be able to keep in mind the larger picture of what you are doing as you become involved in a specific experience.

Although the activities are usually described for one parent and a child, they can be adapted easily for small groups of children. By the same token, they need not be used by parents only. Older brothers and sisters as well as interested grandparents and baby-sitters may find them helpful too.

The activities take place indoors, outside, in the car, at the zoo, in the store. In a very real sense, the whole world is a classroom to explore with your child.

Chapter 1

The Five Senses

Our senses—sight, hearing, touch, taste and smell—bring us information about the world. The degree to which these senses are developed determines the amount of information we can obtain. A painter, for example, has a highly developed sense of sight and an awareness of detail that enables him to reproduce on canvas precisely what he has seen, be it a still life, a gesture or a face. A master chef, on the other hand, concentrates on his sense of taste, so that he can perfectly season his sauces with the right amounts of salt, pepper, lemon and other spices.

And children? They need many experiences with all of their senses; otherwise, their perceptions will be dulled, their vocabulary growth will suffer and their creative instincts will be uninspired.

Children are born explorers. With no prompting whatsoever, they will try to touch, smell, taste, hear and look at whatever is around them. Within reason, let them. Wise parents remove valuable, breakable objects from a young child's reach, so that he will not, in the course of his well-intentioned adventures, frustrate the rest of his family. They cultivate a sense of humor too. Parents who can laugh spontaneously are well equipped to endure and even sympathize with the need of a young child to probe into his world.

For each of his five senses, a preschool child should learn to recognize things that are the "same," and things that are "different." In the case of seeing, for example, he should learn to recognize colors that are the same, shapes that are the same and sizes that are the same. In the case of touch, he should be able to match textures that feel the same: silk with silk, and corduroy with corduroy.

He should learn words that describe sensory qualities: the way things look, sound, taste, feel and smell. For this reason it is important that parents talk about such qualities, introducing words such as "green," "loud," "sour," "smooth," and "smells like vanilla." Soon your preschool child will begin to associate particular sensory qualities with certain things. The sky on a nice day is blue, cows make "moo" sounds, sugar is sweet, velvet is smooth and fried chicken smells like . . . well, fried chicken.

Puzzle play is another aspect of sensory learning. It provides children with an opportunity to talk about pictures and develop visual discrimination skills. A puzzle that is easy for you may be difficult for your child. He may have to study each piece carefully before he perceives its relationship to the whole puzzle. Start your young child on simple puzzles with two or three pieces. Because there are not enough reasonably priced, easy puzzles on the market, you may decide to make them yourself. There is an activity in this chapter that tells how. As your child outgrows one puzzle, make him a new one with a slightly greater challenge. Keep in mind that it takes a certain amount of maturity and puzzle experience before a child can put together a complicated puzzle.

Activity Chart / The Five Senses

Activity	What It Teaches
touch and tell	identifying an object by the sense of touch
sound studio	identifying objects by their characteristic sounds
color cards	naming colors, how to create your own play equipment
1. call the color	recognizing and labeling colors
2. designs	using colors and patterns creatively
3. memory	matching identical colors, remembering colors, following visual directions
4. go fish	recognizing and naming colors, collecting a set of a certain color, following visual and auditory directions
songs of sounds	identifying familiar animal and transportation sounds, expressing sounds musically
blindman's lunch	identifying food by using only the senses of smell and taste
shape-ups	visual discrimination, recognizing and labeling familiar shapes, using shapes creatively
puzzle play	recognizing and relating parts of a picture, visual discrimination
pick-a-pair	tactile discrimination, matching similar textures
curiosity walks	developing one's awareness, using all five senses of perception
sensory riddles	describing the sensory qualities of an object, recognizing an object by its sensory qualities, verbal expression

Touch and Tell

use only your hands to guess what's inside

Materials

a large cardboard box
scissors
tape (the wider, the better)
assorted small objects of various textures:
   spoon, plastic cup, stone, sponge, straw, mitten,
   crayon, silk scarf, small toy, sock

Instructions

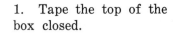

1. Tape the top of the box closed.

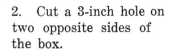

2. Cut a 3-inch hole on two opposite sides of the box.

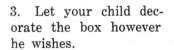

3. Let your child decorate the box however he wishes.

How to play

Fill the box with several objects. Place the box in front of your child so that he can reach—but not see—into it. The object of the game is to identify each object by feeling it. Once your child has named the object, he pulls it out to see if he is correct.

Sound Studio

listen and learn

Materials

tape recorder

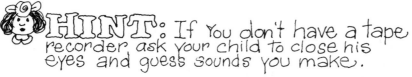

HINT: If you don't have a tape recorder, ask your child to close his eyes and guess sounds you make.

Activity

If you're lucky enough to have a tape recorder, use it to make a tape of sounds for your child to identify. Let him watch as you make it—this way he'll understand where the sounds on the tape originated. Some interesting sounds to try are:

familiar voices	window being opened	alarm clock going off	someone singing
clocks ticking	footsteps	telephone ringing	car screeching
water running	egg beater	dog barking	bicycle bell
refrigerator door being shut	electric shaver	cat meowing	horn blowing

Color Cards

learn as you make them

Materials

an old deck of playing cards (not plastic coated) or 3-inch by 5-inch index cards

colored construction paper (most variety stores sell an inexpensive pack of colored paper that has all of the colors a child should know)

paste, glue or tape (tape that's sticky on both sides works well)

Instructions

1. Cut the colored paper into small rectangles that are the same size as the playing cards or index cards. Cut 4 rectangles of each color. If your child can use scissors, let him help you cut. If not, talk with him about the colors as he watches you.

2. Paste the colored rectangles onto the cards.

3. When you're done, your child will have a deck of color cards to play all of the games described on the next page.

HINT: Clear plastic sandwich boxes provide handy storage for the cards.

Games with Color Cards

who wants to play?

1

This is a simple color recognition game. Mix up the cards and then have your child turn them over one by one, naming each color as he sees it.

2

Encourage your child to be creative with the color cards. Ask: "How many different ways can you lay out the cards?" "What designs can you make?"

3

In this game your child matches colors that are the same. From a pile of cards, he first draws one card, looks at it, names it and puts it color-side down on the table. Remembering what the color was, he tries to find something else in the room that is the same color. If he forgets the color, he may go back and peek at the card.

4

Each player gets 5 cards, which he arranges by color. The object is to get a full set (4) of any color. Players sit in a circle, with the rest of the cards in the middle. The first asks the one on his left "Do you have a red?" If he does, he must hand it over. If not, he says "Go fish." The player then draws from the pack. If he gets the card he wants, he shows it and earns another turn. The first to get a full set wins.

Songs of Sounds

with an oink, oink here and an oink, oink there

Both of these songs can be adapted to sounds that your child knows. If you take a trip to the zoo, add zoo sounds to "Old MacDonald."

Old MacDonald (traditional words and music)

Old MacDonald had a farm,
Ee-i-ee-i-o.
And on his farm, he had a (cow) (Name any animal)
Ee-i-ee-i-o.

With a (moo) , (moo) here,
And a (moo) , (moo) there,
Here a (moo) , there a (moo) ,
Everywhere a (moo-moo) .

Old MacDonald had a farm,
Ee-i-ee-i-o.

Other animals and their sounds:

chicken (cluck)   dog (bow-wow)
duck (quack)   rooster (cock-a-doodle)
pig (oink)   cat (meow)
lamb (baa)   bird (tweet)
horse (neigh)   lion (roar)

The Bus Song (tune: "Mulberry Bush")

The people in the bus go up and down
Up and down, up and down.
The people in the bus go up and down,
All around the town.

Other verses (make them up)

The wiper on the bus goes, swish, swish, swish, etc.
The brake on the bus goes, roomp, roomp, roomp, etc.
The money in the bus goes, clink, clink, clink, etc.
The wheels on the bus go round and round, etc.
The baby on the bus goes, wah, wah, wah, etc.

16

Blindman's Lunch

a game for the senses of smell and taste

Activity

Prepare a lunch that has several distinct tastes and smells—do this when your child isn't watching. When lunchtime arrives, ask your child if he wants to play a special guessing game. If he says yes, blindfold him with a handkerchief. At the table, he tries to guess what food he is eating.

Some tasty menus

peanut butter and jelly
   sandwich
chocolate milk
peach

tuna fish sandwich
lemonade
applesauce

hot dog, mustard, ketchup
celery and carrot sticks
root beer
banana

egg salad sandwich
vanilla milkshake
orange

toast, both dry and
   buttered
tomato soup
milk
chocolate pudding

cheese sandwich, half
   grilled, half plain
prune juice
lemon cookies

Shape-Ups

ways to learn about shapes

Search for Shapes
They're all around. Point them out to your child and soon he'll point them out to you.

Circles

Wheels, balloons, the sun, the moon, eye glasses, balls, bubbles, bowls, glasses, plates, clocks, cups, yo-yos, coins, street lights, hoops.

Rectangles

Doors, windows, barns, apartment houses, trucks, mailboxes, cereal boxes, books, beds, pictures, posters, tables, signs.

Squares

paper napkins, handkerchiefs, windows, chairs, pillows, books, toys, houses, table tops.

Triangles

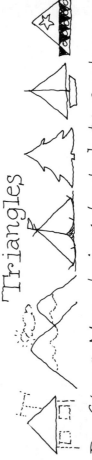

Roof tops, Mountains, tents, hats, sawhorses, Christmas trees, arrow heads, sailboat sails.

HINT: crackers come in circles, squares, rectangles, and *triangles*.

Psychedelic Shapes

Give your child some paper, crayons and shapes to trace. Plastic containers make wonderful round shapes; small boxes provide rectangles and squares, but triangles are hard to come by. You'll probably have to cut them out of heavy cardboard.

Let your child trace each shape over and over, making pretty designs on the paper.

Hang up the artwork so that your child will get a chance to show it to others and to point out the various shapes in the design.

Shape Doodles

Draw the outline of a shape and let your child make the shape into anything he wants. If you outline a circle, he may decide to make the circle into a clown's face or a sun or whatever. Trade roles. Let your child draw the initial shape and you doodle it into something he can recognize.

19

Puzzle Play

with homemade puzzles

1. Gather materials: color pictures from old calendars, postcards and magazines; cardboard (shirt cards are perfect), glue, scissors.

3. Cut the puzzle into puzzle pieces, easy or hard ones depending on your child's age and abilities.

2. Paste the pictures on the cardboard. Paste thoroughly. The better you paste, the better the puzzle.

4. Put it together.

Variation: Have a snapshot of your child's favorite toys blown up. Paste it down carefully on sturdy cardboard (or thin plywood if you have a jigsaw). Cut into puzzle pieces. A wonderful gift.

Pick-a-Pair

a feeling and matching game

Materials

2 medium-small paper bags

2 pieces (each about 2 inches square) of various textures: sandpaper, cotton flannel, foil, corrugated cardboard, sponge, corduroy, silk, brown wrapping paper, plastic (cut from tops of food containers), old washcloths

Instructions

Separate the texture pairs, putting each mate in a different bag. For example, one piece of sandpaper goes in Bag A, the other in Bag B.

Activity
1. Child reaches into Bag A (without peeking) and pulls out a texture piece.

2. Child reaches into Bag B and tries to find the matching texture by feeling.

3. Child lays both pieces together on the table, and starts again, finding a new texture pair.

21

Curiosity Walks

an event of awareness

Take a curiosity walk with your child, *but . . .*

Pick a time when you have time. *Don't* try to get somewhere, *don't* hurry, *don't* press forward. Just relax and be curious—wherever you are: in a park, on a street, in a big department store. Your only objective is to look, listen, touch, smell and hear everything you can. Follow your senses, talk about what they tell you.

What *you* can do:

Follow your child's initiative. Resist the impulse to say, "Hurry up, come along."

Build upon your child's interests. Watch what attracts him. Ask relevant questions: "What is it?" "How does it feel?" "How does it smell?" "Does it make any noise?"

Talk about what the two of you experience. Supply interesting descriptive words: soft, loud, squishy, enormous, bumpy.

HINT:
Your child may be better at this than you.
Watch him. Learn from him.

Later . . . You and your child can talk about, draw about, sing about and laugh about what you did together. Curiosity walks do more than just give curiosity a chance; they provide a unique and special experience for a parent and a child to share.

WHAT DOES IT
FEEL LIKE ?

DOES IT MAKE A
NOISE ?

Sensory Riddles

based on as many senses as possible

This quiet guessing game is fun when riding in the car. You, or whoever is "it," think of something, and make a riddle about it, using as many of the five senses as possible. Whoever guesses the answer is "it" for the next riddle.

What is small, furry and says: MEOW?

What is yellow, gooey, moist, hot to taste, and eaten with hot dogs?

What feels like water, comes in small fancy bottles, and smells beautiful?

What has numbers on a dial and goes "RING, RING"?

What smells fresh and clean, makes suds, and tastes terrible?

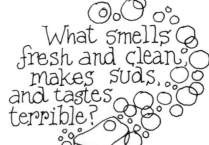

What is brown, squishy, and fun to walk through?

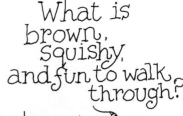

Chapter 2

Language Development

One of the most dramatic and remarkable accomplishments that occurs in the first four years of a child's growth is the acquisition of language. The average child knows about two thousand words by the time he is five. Furthermore, he can understand and use the basic sentence structures of our language in a remarkably sophisticated way —an amazing accomplishment.

Just exactly how a child learns to understand and speak a language is not completely clear. Child experts, educational psychologists and linguists have various theories and continue to search for keys to a more thorough understanding of the process. Why do some children learn to talk before others? Why do some gain a greater mastery over words and sentences? We do not yet fully know. But there are some aspects of language learning of which we can be relatively sure.

First of all, we know that children need lots of experience with words and with language. They need to hear all kinds of words.

> Words like street, car and window—that tell what they see
> Words like run, cry and laugh—that tell what they do
> Words like soft, pretty and old—that tell how things look
> Words like grumpy, happy and sad—that tell how they feel

It is not surprising that in homes where children are spoken to rarely, language development is hampered. And, conversely, in homes where parents talk interestedly to their children about where they are, what they are doing and how they are feeling, verbal development flows. Children learn to talk and listen. You see mothers and children in the supermarkets, chatting about fruits and vegetables. You see them paused at a new construction site talking about cranes and dump trucks. This instinct for conversation is a great asset for parents, since it is often the very act of verbalizing a thought or activity that clinches learning.

Secondly, we know that children need to hear language patterns. Parents supply the patterns when they talk with their children. When your child points to his ball and says, "ball," you may know that he wants you to hand him the ball. You can point to the ball and say, "Ball? Do you want the ball? Can you say, 'Give me the ball'?" As you hand him the ball you can say, "Here's the ball." The child who hears sentences often will be likely to develop *sentence sense.* He will start linking words together in the same sentence patterns that he hears adults using.

Thirdly, we know that this is the time that children most love to listen to the sounds of language. Children at this age love nursery rhymes even when they don't understand them. They simply delight in the sound of words —in rhythm and rhyme. Read aloud. Read favorites over and over again.

Finally, we know that children need practice using languge. They need to be encouraged to experiment. The play/learning activities in this chapter are planned to help you have fun together while your child is learning new words and practicing using language.

Activity Chart / Language Development

Activity	What It Teaches
tips on talking with children	suggestions and guidelines for parents to follow when talking with their children
touch and talk	associating words with objects
play cards	associating words and pictures with real things identifying rhyming words identifying initial sounds using context clues
a time for listening	suggestions for parents about the kinds of things children at this age like to hear
questions	using words to ask questions
yes, no, maybe	using sentences to answer questions
riddle dee dee	using words to describe using context clues finding words that rhyme
my dog Sunshine	associating words with actions using context clues
puppets	using words to tell a story putting a story into your own words
silly sentences	developing sentence sense

Tips on Talking with Children

or with adults—the art of conversation remains the same

Keep it natural. Don't talk your child to death. Too much talk can take the joy and spontaneity out of an experience.

Be sure your interest is real. Youngsters are quicker than adults when it comes to knowing a phony. Try sharing what really interests you. You may be surprised at how your child responds.

Ask questions—real questions. "How did it make you feel—happy or sad?" "Which do you like best?" "Why do you like it best?" "What would you do?" "What color do you want?"

Go deeper. Follow up on your child's comments and questions.

Don't talk down. Conversation is a person-to-person event. Anything less is bound to feel flat. If the difference in size is a problem, kneel, squat or sit so that you are eye to eye while you talk.

Be direct. If you don't feel like talking or explaining—say so. Say, "I'm too busy to talk now, but I will explain after dinner before you go to bed." Or, "I'd like to hear about your picture, but I can't take time to listen now. I hope you'll tell me about it before you go to bed tonight." Be sure you follow up on whatever you suggest—even if you have to be the one to bring it up.

Listen.

30

Touch and Talk

an all-the-time, everywhere game

At bath time . . .
Touch and name each part of the body as you help your child wash.

As you dress your child . . .
Talk with your child about his clothes as you help him dress.

As you cook . . .
Talk about what you are doing.

"Scrub one knee. What am I scrubbing?"

"My knee!"

"Yes, I'm scrubbing your knee. And what's this funny thing at the end of your leg?"

"A foot!"

"Yes, a foot. Your right foot. Scrub one foot."

"What color sweater do you want to wear? Your red sweater or your blue sweater?"

"Put your arm through here. What's this part called?"

"The sleeve."

"Yes. Put your arm through the sleeve."

"First I'll peel the carrots, and then I'll slice them. Am I making the slices as thin as I can? Would you like a slice to taste?"

Play Cards

you can't have too many

Materials

picture magazines
old postcards and greet-
  ing cards
inexpensive coloring
  books
index cards (large size,
  5-inch by 8-inch,
  unlined are best)
scissors
paste
crayons
Optional: A shoe box for
  storage

Instructions

Look through the
magazines, post-
cards, greeting
cards, coloring
books and any-
thing else you
have handy or
think of that has
lots of pictures.

1. Cut out the pictures of the things
your child likes best—a dog, a
truck, a house, a man—
and paste them on index cards.

2. Be sure that
each card
shows only
one thing.
Print the
name of the
thing on
the card.

3. If possible, find more than one
picture of each thing. Paste each
picture on a separate card, but
print the same label. Seeing more
than one kind of the same thing—
such as several kinds of trucks or
several kinds of dogs—will help
broaden your child's concepts.

Games with Play Cards

everything has a name

Match

Collect pictures of things in your house such as a picture of a chair, a picture of a stove, a picture of a baby. Place the cards face up on the table. Point to one card at a time and ask your child if he can find a real thing that matches the picture.

Play the game again, only this time you point to the real thing and ask your child to pick out the matching picture card.

Pickup

Place the cards face up on a table. Make up a riddle about one of the things on the picture cards. Ask your child to point to the card that answers the riddle. Say, "Pick up a picture of something that rhymes with pot." "Pick up a picture of something that starts with the same sound as mother." "Pick up a picture of something that is made of wood."

Draw a Sentence

Use play cards to play a sentence game. Put the cards picture-side down. The player picks 3 cards and turns them picture-side up. If he can make a sentence using the things on his cards, he keeps them, if not, the next player tries. Keep playing until all cards have been won. If the cards were a boat, a cat and a man, the sentence might be: "I saw a cat riding with a man in a boat" or: "A man carried his cat to a boat."

33

A Time for Listening

learning by imitating

A child learns language by imitating what he hears. Be sure your child has lots of chances to listen. He'll want to hear the same thing over and over again. That's fine—it's an important part of learning language; but be sure that he has new things to listen to as well.

Whenever possible, read aloud to your child. Listening to the sound of your voice, hearing new words and hearing the words he knows used in new ways are all important parts of learning to use language.

Poetry delights children at this age. Read short poems like those found in Mother Goose and long narrative ones like *Wynken, Blynken, and Nod.* This is the time to introduce tongue twisters and the wonderful rhyme and nonsense sounds of Dr. Seuss.

Don't forget . . . there are many children's records you can buy or borrow from the library.

Questions

guess what I'm thinking

Activity

Think of something both you and your child know. Your pet dog. Your car. Your dentist. The clock on the kitchen wall. It can be anything as long as it's something your child knows well.

Start by saying, "I'm thinking of something. Your job is to find out what it is I'm thinking of by asking me questions. Tell me when you think you know what it is and we'll stop the game. If you guess what I'm thinking, you win, and it will be your turn to be 'it.'"

At first you may want to help him think of good questions. Ask, "Would it help if you knew whether or not I was thinking of a person? What question could you ask to find out if it's a person?"

Or you may want to give some clues: "It's someone we know." "It's something you see every day." "It's something you use when it's cold outside."

Yes, No, Maybe

answering questions

Take turns asking questions. The only rule of the game is that you can't use the words "yes," "no" or "maybe" when you answer.

Q. "Are your eyes blue?"
A. "My eyes are not blue."
Q. "Would you like an ice-cream cone?"
A. "I would very much like an ice-cream cone."

Riddle Dee Dee

a waiting game

Activity

Pull some riddles out of your sleeve when you and your child are waiting for things to happen—the dentist to call you into his office, the car trip to be over, dinner to be served.

Animal Riddles

I eat grass
I say moo
Who am I?

I gallop
I trot
My hooves go clip-clop
Who am I?

I have feathers
I peck and peck
I say cluck, cluck, cluck
Who am I?

Rhyming Riddles

I say moo
I rhyme with sow
Who am I?

I have a trunk
I rhyme with knee
Who am I?

Just Plain Riddles

I'm red and white
I have a tail
I'm made of paper
I fly high in the sky
Who am I?

I'm red
I'm juicy
You eat me sliced, with salt and pepper
Who am I?

Hint: Don't try to make them fancy or tricky. Make them easy. Even young children will soon catch on and join in the fun.

My Dog Sunshine

a sign language game

Activity: Tell a story leaving out certain words. Use sign language to give the meaning of the missing words and let your child fill in the missing words.

Story		**Motion**

My dog Sunshine walked _____ the bridge.

Make *over* action with your hand.

She ran _____ the hill.

Make *down* action with your hand.

The story continues: under the fence, up the hill, around the block.

Variation: Play the same game leaving out action words such as walk, run, skip, jump, hop. Act out the word you are leaving out for your child to guess.

Puppets

made from socks, apples and paper bags

Children blossom with chatter when called on to provide speech for puppets they have made. When a child plays with a puppet, he has a chance to act out both sides of a conversation. He has a chance to put the stories he knows into his own words. He has a chance to play the part of his favorite character. He can act out for himself the things he has seen on television. He can play the part of parents or friends.

While you might need to get things started by suggesting that he act out a favorite story, chances are he'll need little or no direction once he has the finished puppet in hand.

It's not important that puppets be fancy—what is important is that they be easy and quick to make. Look over the following varieties and pick the one that best suits your child and your supplies.

Stick Puppets

Stuff a paper bag with crushed newspaper. Slip a stick or cardboard paper-towel roll part way into the paper bag. Tie the bag at the neck with a piece of string. Draw the puppet's face on a separate piece of paper, cut it out and paste it on the paper bag. Glue on yarn or paper curls for hair.

Hand Puppets

Draw a face on a tiny paper bag. Cut a hole for a finger nose. Your thumb and middle finger become arms.

In a hollow ball, cut a hole just large enough to insert a cardboard paper-towel roll. The roll should extend below the head so that clothes can be attached. Draw a face on the ball with felt-tip markers.

Enlarge the pattern on the left to fit your puppet. Cut two pieces from fabric. Sew or glue together, leaving the neck, armholes and hem open. Decorate with scraps of lace, fur, fringe, buttons, feathers, tassels and ribbon or anything else you have on hand. Attach the costume to the neck of the puppet with glue or string.

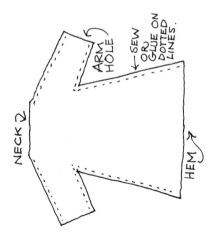

NECK

ARM HOLE

← SEW OR GLUE ON DOTTED LINES.

HEM →

NOW, YOU'VE VERY VERY BEEN A VERY LITTLE NAUGHTY JUST SO GIRL, AND DO IT YOU WON'T YOU CAN'T AGAIN, YOU FOR! WATCH TV WEEK! ONE WHOLE WEEK. SO THERE.

Stage A decorated cardboard carton or small table will do.

Silly Sentences

everybody adds on to make a silly story

Activity

Start a sentence: "I saw a cow sitting . . ."

Ask your child to finish the sentence: ". . . in the middle of our kitchen. The cow was eating a piece of apple pie. She was as fat as . . ."

Then it's your turn to repeat and add on: "I saw a cow sitting in the middle of our kitchen. The cow was eating . . ."

Your child finishes it: ". . . a piece of apple pie."

You repeat it all and go on: "I saw a cow sitting in the middle of our kitchen. The cow was eating a piece of apple pie. She was as fat as . . ."

After he catches on, make repeating the first part of the story an important part of the game.

Hint: Use open-ended comparisons to encourage your child's imagination: The man was as tall as . . . The kitten was as soft as . . .

Chapter 3

Prereading

There are lots of things you can do to help your child get ready to read. In this chapter we have focused on activities and experiences that will help a child learn the skills that provide a foundation for learning to read. There are games to help him learn the letters of the alphabet. There are play experiences that will make your child want to read. There are games to help him learn that words stand for real things and a game that will simply help him learn to find the top and bottom of a page. These are all things that a child needs to know before he can learn to read—experiences that will make it easier for him to read when the time comes.

You've probably wondered *if* you should teach your preschool child to read. Whatever you decide, you'll find expert opinions to support your position. It is our opinion that the right answer depends on your child. You know your child. You can best decide whether or not your child is ready. What one child learns at four, another learns at six. This doesn't mean that one child is more intelligent than the other—it means that children are different. Children learn different things at different times. What *is* important is that you're sure that you're not pushing your child to learn something he's not ready for. If your child resists, he's probably not ready. Keep in mind that success is the key to learning. If your child fails in his first reading attempts he'll not want to try again. On the other hand, if you wait until he's ready, you'll be setting the stage for a successful and rewarding experience.

Activity Chart / Prereading

Activity	What It Teaches
mystery picture	using picture clues, using context clues
doodles	recognizing different points of view, using picture clues
learning letters	suggestions for parents about making the alphabet more meaningful
letter puzzlers	recognizing the parts that make a letter, comparing letters, seeing how they are the same and how they are different
sandpaper letters:	
1. what did you catch?	identifying and naming letters of the alphabet
2. alphabet lotto	comparing letters, recognizing and matching letters that are the same
alphabet line:	
1. pin-up	recognizing and matching letters that are the same
2. line-up	identifying letters of the alphabet and putting them in order
3. hang-up	recognizing initial sounds and matching sounds with letters
4. words	using letters to make words
a picture dictionary	associating pictures, words and letters, listening for and identifying initial sounds, matching letters and sounds
learning to print the alphabet	guidelines and suggestions for parents about teaching children to print

name nuts	associating words with real things, associating spoken and written words
pictures tell stories	understanding that pictures tell stories, developing story sense
picture strips	using pictures and words to tell a story, identifying a sequence of events, putting a story into your own words
name game	identifying and matching initial sounds
giant page	identifying the parts of a page, following directions
directions	following directions, remembering
a reading corner	suggestions for parents about developing a child's love of stories, reading and books

story time:
1. reading aloud
2. making up stories

books: understanding and appreciating books, understanding that books are stories written down

1. dictate a story
2. comic books
    abridged
3. picture book
4. photographs

more about books   two different ways to make your own

Mystery Picture

what is it?

Materials
large envelope
magazines
heavy paper
scissors
glue or paste

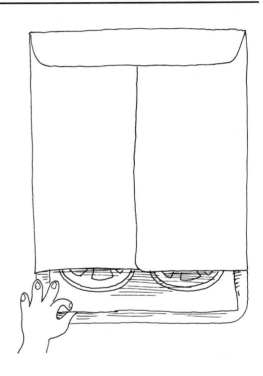

Activity
Look through magazines for pictures of things your child knows: trucks, cars, animals, people—anything. Cut out the pictures and paste each one on a separate piece of paper. Put the picture in the envelope so that the bottom of the picture will come out of the envelope first.

Pull the first picture out of the envelope just far enough for your child to see the bottom. Ask, "What do you see? Two wheels? What do you think the picture can be? A dog? No?" Pull the picture a little farther out of the envelope so that new clues appear. Continue the game until your child guesses what the picture is.

Doodles

help your child think of different points of view

Materials
crayons
paper

Activity
Doodles are a wonderful way to help children think of things from a different point of view.

A table

from beside

from above

A tree

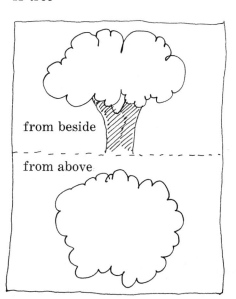

from beside

from above

A hamburger

from beside

from above

Learning Letters

take a moment to think about why

The letters of the alphabet are important because we put them together to make words. Many children can recite the alphabet, but have no idea of what it means. It's important for you to find ways to help your child understand the purpose of letters. Learning letters is more fun when the letters make up your child's name or when they spell his favorite cereal. Whenever you can, take time to help your child look for letters he knows:

on traffic signs	in the newspaper you're reading
in street names	on cereal boxes
on book covers	on cans
on television	in the letter you are writing

HINT: An old typewriter is a wonderful teaching machine. So is the new hand letter-punch gadget. Both the typewriter and the punch provide an opportunity for children to make words out of letters — an important language experience.

Letter Puzzlers

shapes make letters

Materials
cardboard or heavy paper
scissors

Instructions
Cut out shapes that make letters:
    Straight lines—long and short
    Half circles—big and little

Activity
Give your child a few shapes at a time. Start with two straight lines—one long, one short—and a small half circle. Ask, "What letters can you make with these pieces?"

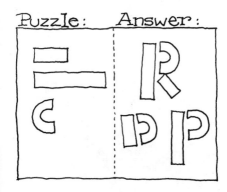

Puzzle: Answer:

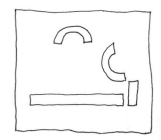

VARIATION:

Use the shapes to start a picture. Place several shapes on a piece of paper. Say, "This is the beginning of a picture. Can you finish my picture?"

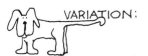

49

Sandpaper Letters

getting the "feel" of the alphabet

Materials

light- or medium-weight sandpaper
scissors
alphabet stencil (with large, simple letters)
glue
linoleum or cardboard squares for backing

Instructions

1. Trace the letters on the smooth side of the sandpaper. Be sure to reverse them—tracing the letters backwards—so that the sandpaper surface will show correct letters.

2. Cut out the letters.

3. Glue sandpaper to heavy cardboard or squares of linoleum. You can cut out the letters if you want to, but it isn't necessary. They will be raised slightly from the surface and easy to feel because of their rough surface.

Activity

Help your child trace the shape of each letter with his finger as you talk about it. Say, "See the letter A. The letter A is made of three straight lines. One, two and the third connecting them."

Place a few letters in a paper bag. Ask, "Can you find me the letter A without looking?"

50

Games with Sandpaper Letters

1. What Did You Catch?

Place the sandpaper letters on a table or on the floor, rough-side up. Attach a paper clip to each letter. Make a fishing pole from a stick and string, with a horseshoe magnet tied at the end of the string. Let your child fish for the letters. When he gets one (or more), ask, "What did you catch?" After he tells you the name of the letter, put it aside and fish for another. Keep playing until he's caught all the letters.

2. Alphabet Lotto

Materials
large piece of paper
ruler
crayons

Instructions
Divide the large piece of paper into 26 spaces, the same size as the sandpaper letters. Print a letter in each square. It's more fun if you don't write the letters in order.

Activity
Cover each square on the paper with the matching alphabet card.

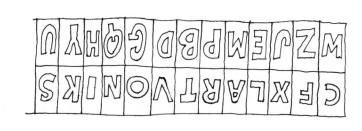

Alphabet Line

mix them up, hang them up

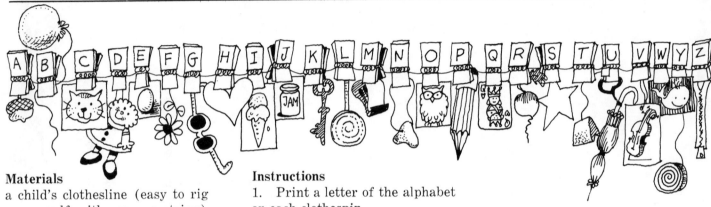

Materials

a child's clothesline (easy to rig
yourself with rope or string)
clothespins (at least 26)
a collection of real things (or pictures of things) for each letter
(Don't worry about finding things
that begin with X or Z—there
aren't many. Do be ready to help
your child hear the sound of X
in such words as exit, extra
and next, and the letter Z whenever you come across it.)
paper (at least 26 pieces)

Instructions

1. Print a letter of the alphabet
on each clothespin.
2. Write each letter of the alphabet on a separate piece of paper.

Activities

1. *Pin-up*

Lay the pieces of paper with the
letters written on them on the floor
—out of order. Put the clothespins
on the line in order. Ask, "Can
you hang up the letters of the
alphabet in the right order?"

2. *Hang-up*

Look for real things to hang from
each clothespin. Point out the difference between the letter's name
and its sound. "The name of this
letter is B. It sounds like 'ba':
banana, Band-Aid, boy."

3. *Words*

Use the clothespin letters to make
words. "Can you spell your name?"

A Picture Dictionary

how many pictures can you find to go with each letter?

Instructions

1. Fold paper to make a book with a minimum of 26 pages. (See *More About Books*, page 66.)
2. Use a crayon or felt-tip marker to print a letter of the alphabet in the corner of each page.

Activity

Illustrate the book. Look for pictures of things that begin with each letter. Try to find several pictures to go with each letter and paste them on the appropriate page. Print the name of each picture. Adding pictures and words can be an ongoing project.

Materials

a scrap book of large pieces of paper
crayons or felt-tip markers
magazines, postcards, old greeting cards
scissors
paste or glue

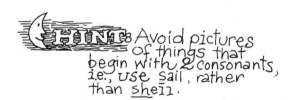

HINT: Avoid pictures of things that begin with 2 consonants, i.e., use sail, rather than shell.

Learning to Print the Alphabet

and your very own name

Materials
crayons and lots of paper or
blackboard and lots of chalk

Should you teach your child to print? It's up to you. If he wants to learn, then he's probably ready. If he seems to lose interest when you start to show him how to make a letter, then stop. Don't force him. He probably isn't ready to learn.

It isn't necessary to learn the letters in order. You'll probably want to start by teaching your child how to print his name with all capital letters. Show him how to make one letter at a time. You might say, "The letter A is made of three lines. One line slants like this (make the line). The second line starts at the same place and slants like this (make the line). The third line is a short line that joins the other two like this (make the line)."

Let him try making the letter while you watch. Then give him lots of time to practice on his own.

This chart shows the standard way to make each letter. The arrows indicate the direction of the stroke. The numbers indicate the order in which the strokes are made. Before you teach your child, check the chart so that you can be sure he's learning the right way to make each letter from the start.

Name Nuts

label everything in sight

Materials
index cards, 5-inch by 3-inch
crayons or felt-tip markers
string or masking tape

Activity
Say, "We're going to play a naming game. Do you want
to be a name nut? We'll see how many things in this
room we can name. What's the first thing you want to
name? Table. I'll print the word *table* on this card."
Help your child tape or tie it to the object. Continue in
this way making labels for everything:

refrigerator	coat	door
sister	dog	window
mommy	toothbrush	curtain
bread	bathtub	car
closet	boat	wagon

Later, print the same words on another set of cards.
Place the cards face up on the floor and say, "Which of
these words do you know? If you think you know a
word, take it to the thing it goes with and see if it is
the same as the label." Your child can keep the ones he
knows. (A shoe box is a good place to store them.)

HINTS:

Masking tape can be easily removed
from some surfaces. In those places,
write the word directly on the masking
tape.

Read everything in your sight to your
child... signs, labels, cereal boxes, words
on T.V. Read aloud to him often.
See "Language Development", page 27, 28.

56

Pictures Tell Stories

when you put them in order

Materials

old comic books or
   ready-to-be-discarded picture books
scissors
paste or glue
heavy paper or cardboard

Instructions

Comic books are a good place to find picture sequences that tell a story. While you may start out with a two-picture sequence, a three-to-five-picture sequence is best. If you can find pictures that can be arranged in different sequences to tell several stories—all the better.
If finding a series of pictures that work together is a problem, you might help your child draw a sequence of pictures that tell a favorite story.

Activity

Place a sequence of pictures on the table or on the floor—out of order. Ask, "Can you use these pictures to tell a story? Put them in order so that they tell your story." Be ready to accept any story that your child can logically explain—even if it is not the original story that went with the pictures.

For example:
(1) sad boy

(2) sad dog

(3) happy boy
and happy dog
together

Picture Strips

to tell your favorite story

Materials
paper—a roll of shelf paper is ideal. As a substitute,
   tape pieces of paper together to make a strip
crayons
adhesive or masking tape

Activity
Try making picture strips to tell a favorite story. The finished strip can be hung on the wall for decoration. If you darken the room, you can spotlight the pictures with a flashlight as your child narrates. This is a good follow-up activity for your child after he has taken a trip or been on a vacation.

Name Game

a good car game

Activity

This is a question-and-answer game that children enjoy playing. Help your child think of things that start with the same letter and the same sound as his name.

Q: What's your name?
A: My name is Billy.
Q: Where do you live?
A: I live in Baltimore.
Q: What do you eat?
A: I eat bananas.

Other questions: "What sport do you like?" "What do you like to wear?" "What's your favorite dessert?" "What's your favorite animal?"

Continue the game with other names. Say, "I know a girl named Mary. Where do you think she lived?"
  "Maine!"
  "Yes. Mary lived in Maine," and so on.

Giant Page

learning your way around a page

Materials

a large, sturdy piece of paper (it should be at least 2 feet by 3 feet—a brown paper bag opened out is about the right size)

adhesive or masking tape

Activity

Open out the paper and tape it to the floor so that it will stay in place. Say, "I've got a new game called Giant Page. Pretend this is a giant page from a giant book!" Introduce the different parts of a page—a few at a time. Start with the top, bottom and middle. At first point to them. Together, make finding them again a game. Say, "See if you can do exactly what I tell you: Point to the center of the page. Stand in the middle of the page."

To make the game more lively, think of funny directions: "Put your elbow on the bottom of the page."

Later go on to more difficult parts:

top left corner

lower right corner

Don't introduce all parts of the page on one day. This is a game to play over and over.

Variation

Make the game still harder. Use two pages. Teach the expressions *left-hand page* and *right-hand page*. Ask, "Find the top right corner of the left-hand page." "Point to the bottom of the right-hand page."

HINT: Is your child having fun? If not, stop.

Directions

listen carefully

Activity

Say, "Let's play the Direction Game. First, listen carefully to everything I say. Then, see if you can do *exactly* as I said."

☆**HINT**: Start with very simple directions. Gradually build to more complicated instructions. The game should be challenging, but never so hard that your child doesn't succeed at following out the majority of your directions.

DIRECTION #1	DIRECTION #2
• HOP TO YOUR CLOSET. • OPEN THE DOOR. • LOOK INSIDE. • CLOSE THE DOOR. • TELL ME ONE THING YOU SAW IN YOUR CLOSET.	• SKIP AROUND THE TABLE. • WHISPER YOUR NAME TWICE. • SIT DOWN. • SMILE.
DIRECTION #3	**DIRECTION #4**
• TOUCH YOUR TOES TWICE. • TOUCH YOUR ELBOW ONCE. • PAT THE TOP OF YOUR HEAD TWICE.	• OPEN THE TOP DRAWER. • LOOK IN THE LEFT HAND CORNER. • CLOSE THE DRAWER. • TELL ME WHAT YOU SAW.

A Reading Corner

a special place for books and reading

Make books and reading an important part of your child's life right from the start. A combination room-divider/bookrack makes a special place for reading. It's inexpensive and easy to make. Furnish the corner with some comfortable pillows and lots of books—your child's and other people's—and magazines.

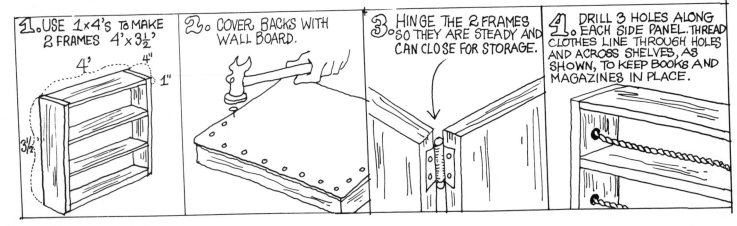

1. USE 1×4's TO MAKE 2 FRAMES 4'×3½'

2. COVER BACKS WITH WALL BOARD.

3. HINGE THE 2 FRAMES SO THEY ARE STEADY AND CAN CLOSE FOR STORAGE.

4. DRILL 3 HOLES ALONG EACH SIDE PANEL. THREAD CLOTHES LINE THROUGH HOLES AND ACROSS SHELVES, AS SHOWN, TO KEEP BOOKS AND MAGAZINES IN PLACE.

Story Time

once a day

Reading Aloud
Be sure to take the time to look through
magazines and books with your child. At
least once a day, try to spend some time
reading together.

Making Up Stories
Your child will delight in thinly disguised
stories about him. He'll happily supply the
plot and the details if you encourage him.
Say, "Once I knew a little boy. Do you know
what that little boy wanted more than anything in the world?" Use whatever your
child suggests. "Yes, he wanted a puppy.
Well, he got a wonderful little puppy." To
continue the story, ask more questions:
"Can you guess what he named it?" "What
do you think happened to that little boy
and his puppy?"

Books

any time is the right time to make your own

The surest way to encourage your child's love for books is to encourage him to write his very own. Help him understand that a book is a story —his story—written down. A child who writes his own books will be more interested in books other people have written. He'll also have a better understanding of what he reads.

What will the book be about?

Chances are your child will have lots of ideas. Be ready to accept whatever your child wants to write about. Withhold literary and moral judgment for a later time. This is the time to encourage self-confidence and free expression.

HINT:

The most important line on the book is the byline. Never, never forget to give it the attention and the emphasis it deserves. If possible, use a Polaroid camera to get a snapshot of the author at work. At the very least, find an old picture of your child to glue on the cover of the book.

Dictate a Story

Write what your child tells you—one sentence to a page—in capital and lower-case letters so it looks just like the print in a book.

You:	"What would you like to make a book about?"
Child:	"My turtle."
You:	"Okay. The title of this book is Anna's Turtle." Print it. "It's by Anna Smith." Print the byline in large letters. "What do you want to say about your turtle?"
Child:	"My turtle is green."
You:	"Okay." Print the sentence: My turtle is green. Read it aloud as you print. Turn to the next page and ask: "Anything else?"
Child:	"Yes. My turtle is named Sam."

The story doesn't have to be long or complex to be a book. What was dictated in the example above is enough.

Comic Books Abridged

Make a new book with pictures from a comic book. Help your child paste them in. Ask him to dictate captions for each. He may retell the comic book story in his own words or make up a new story. It doesn't matter as long as it makes sense.

Picture Book

Simply cut out pictures that you like. It's fun to make a picture book on a topic: Photograph Stories by Emily, Mozella's Book of Round Things, Anna's Turtle.

Photographs

Even youngsters can operate some of the simple new cameras—they're inexpensive and one of the most exciting learning tools you can buy for your child. Show him how to work it and set him free. Each batch of photos can become a photo essay when pasted in a book. He can dictate captions.

More About Books

two different ways to make your own

Materials
paper
string
staples or cellophane tape
crayons or felt-tip markers
paper-puncher

Method I

1. Make single pages; one sheet of paper equals two page sides. Be sure to leave a 1-inch margin on all edges.

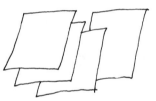

2. When the book is finished, put the pages together in order. Staple along one edge. Or punch two holes along one edge and tie sheets together with a piece of string.

Method II

1. Fold sheets of paper in half. This way each sheet of paper makes four page sides.

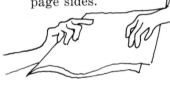

2. Tie in the middle with a piece of string or yarn. To make a sturdier book, punch two holes along center fold and thread string through before tying.

3. Put between two heavy books to crease firmly.

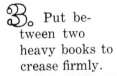

Chapter 4

Understanding Relationships

There is a whole category of words that we commonly use to describe how one thing relates to another. For example, consider the italicized words in the following sentences:

This antenna is *longer* than that one.

The antenna should be *on top of* the TV.

Drive your car *around* the construction area.

It is *nearer* to the post office than it is to the bank.

Make sure you go *before* rush hour.

You carry this box; it's *lighter*.

It is? But it has *more* books.

We use these italicized words to clarify our communication. We describe how long the antenna is by comparing it with another. In the second sentence, the word *around* tells the driver precisely where to drive his car. These words describe relationships—one antenna in comparison with another and the direction of a car in relationship to an obstacle.

Before a child can use a *relationship word*, he has to: (1) learn the actual words, and (2) understand the concept behind them. In other words, understanding relationships is a skill that involves more than vocabulary. Consider the sentences again, keeping in mind the notion of a concept behind each italicized word.

This antenna is *longer* than that one. (concept of size)

The antenna should be *on top of* the TV. (concept of position)

Drive your car *around* the construction area. (concept of direction)

It is *nearer* to the post office than it is to the bank. (concept of distance)

Make sure you go *before* rush hour. (concept of time)

You carry this box; it's *lighter*. (concept of weight)

It is? But it has *more* books. (concept of amount)

In order to develop awareness of a particular concept, a child needs to explore materials that demonstrate it. For example, he might learn the concept of size by playing with measuring cups that nest inside one another. After a variety of such concrete experiences, he will begin to understand the abstract concept of size and such relationship words as *small, smaller* and *smallest*.

Another group of words included in this chapter are the *opposite words*: noisy-quiet, rough-smooth, hot-cold, soft-hard, big-little. Again, basic concepts are important. It is hard to understand the meaning of *hot* without understanding the word *cold*. By experiencing both, a child learns the relationship between the two and can use the words to describe opposite conditions.

Some of the activities in this chapter are experiences with ordering—for example, the activity that consists of drawing family members in a row from the shortest to the tallest. Another exercise is putting glasses of water in order from the most full to the least full. Such activities are related to comparing; in a way, they are the act of comparing one thing with others in a group. The ability to order a series of different objects is an important precursor of arithmetic skills, all of which are based on the idea that numbers are ordered: 1 is smaller than 2, 2 is smaller than 3, 3 is smaller than 4.

Activity Chart / Understanding Relationships

Activity	What It Teaches
hop on the scale	comprehension and use of weight words: light, lighter, lightest; heavy, heavier, heaviest
watch where I go	comprehension and use of direction words: over, under, above, below, up, down, in, out, left, right, forward, backward, sideways
building blocks	comprehension and use of size, shape and position words: big, bigger, biggest; little, littler, littlest; small, smaller, smallest; short, shorter, shortest; tall, taller, tallest; long, longer, longest; thin, thinner, thinnest; fat, fatter, fattest; circle, ball, cylinder, round, square, cube, rectangle, triangle, pyramid; on the bottom, on top of, under, on, in, inside, outside, in the middle, in between, next to, behind, in front of, left, right; how to create your own play equipment
tick-tock	comprehension of time as something that can be measured; understanding that events happen before and after other events
learning in the sandbox	comprehension and use of amount words: same, more, less, most, all, some, none
opposites	comprehension and use of opposite words
ordering	being able to put things in a row from the most to the least (pertaining to size and quantity) and vice versa
nearer, nearer	comprehension and use of distance words: here, there, near, nearer, nearest, far, farther, farthest

Hop on the Scale

the concept of weight

Weigh your toys, your friends, yourself—all on the bathroom scale.

At first, teach your child the weight words by having him lift and compare two or three objects at a time. Once he knows the words, show him the scale, explaining that it tells how much things weigh. Demonstrate how to read numbers and how to record them on a weight chart.

NAME	POUNDS
1. MOMMY	135
2. DADDY	190
3. ME	42
4. JOHN	50
5. RUTHIE	21
6. ROVER	$16\frac{1}{2}$

Weight Words: *light, lighter, lightest heavy, heavier, heaviest*

Who's the heaviest? Lightest?

Watch Where I Go

the concept of direction

Follow the leader with trucks or dolls
You select one truck (or doll) and your child selects another. Take the two on a trip around the room, talking about where you are as you move about. First you be the leader, and then when your child catches on, let him have a try.

OVER GRANDMA!

UNDER THE TABLE!

UNDER THE CHAIR!

UNDER THE RUG!

OVER THE PLANT!

TO THE LEFT OF THE LAMP!

BACKWARDS!

FORWARD!

Building Blocks

the concepts of size, shape and position

HOW TO MAKE YOUR OWN BLOCKS:

Materials
milk and cream
   cartons, all sizes
tape
paint

Directions
1. Cut the tops off two cartons the same size.

2. Fit the cartons together.

3. Tape them shut.

4. Decorate with paint.

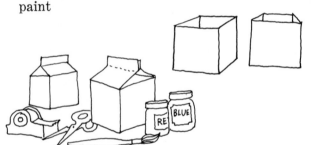
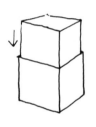

HINT:
ADD DETERGENT
TO PAINT
TO MAKE IT STICK!

Tip on purchasing commercially made blocks
Blocks are made in a variety of materials: wood, plastic, foam and cardboard. Children seem to prefer wood, perhaps because it feels so nice. The main disadvantage of wooden blocks is expense. Two ways to combat high cost are: (1) make the blocks yourself from lumber scraps (your children can help), and (2) buy a set of *small* wooden table top blocks—ideally suited for apartments and small homes.

IS THE TRAIN GOING UNDER OR OVER THE BRIDGE?

Learning with blocks

The words listed below can be learned through play. How? By using them naturally in conversations with your child as he plays with his blocks. "Which block is taller? Which one is behind you? Which block is round?"

SIZE WORDS

BIG, BIGGER, BIGGEST
LITTLE, LITTLER, LITTLEST
SMALL, SMALLER, SMALLEST
SHORT, SHORTER, SHORTEST
TALL, TALLER, TALLEST
LONG, LONGER, LONGEST
THIN, THINNER, THINNEST
FAT, FATTER, FATTEST

SHAPE WORDS

CIRCLE
BALL
CYLINDER
ROUND
SQUARE, CUBE
RECTANGLE
TRIANGLE
PYRAMID

POSITION WORDS

ON TOP OF
ON THE BOTTOM
UNDER   BEHIND

          IN THE MIDDLE NEXT TO
          IN BETWEEN
          IN FRONT OF
LEFT   RIGHT
              ON
              IN
          INSIDE
          OUTSIDE

75

Opposites

learn them together

An easy way to teach a word is to teach its opposite at the same time. If a ball goes up, it must come down—and right away you have two words to talk about.

ON OFF

SHADE

LIGHT

SAD

NIGHT DAY

BOY GIRL

HAPPY

Tick-Tock

the concept of time

YOU CAN WATCH TV AFTER DINNER

"MAKE A CLOCK"

1. FASTEN PAPER HANDS TO PAPER PLATE WITH GOLD FASTENER OR STRING.

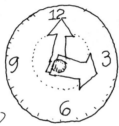

2. ADD NUMBERS. START WITH 12, 3, 6 AND 9. FILL IN THE REST.

"KEEP A DAILY SCHEDULE"

MY DAY

7:30 - GET UP
7:45 - EAT BREAKFAST
8:00 - PLAY
9:00 - NURSERY SCHOOL
12:00 - LUNCH
1:00 - NAP
2:00 - PLAY
5:30 - SUPPER
6:00 - PLAY AND STORY TIME
7:30 - BED TIME

"THREE"

COO COO

Learning in the Sandbox

the concept of amount

Next time your child goes to his sandbox or to the beach, give him some paper cups to play with. Help him use these cups in a learning game. Fill them with varying amounts of sand, talking casually about the amount in each cup. Ask questions that involve comparisons:

Which cup has more sand?

Which cup has less sand?

Which cup has all the sand?

Which cup has none?

AMOUNT WORDS: SAME, MORE, LESS, MOST, ALL, SOME, NONE

79

Ordering

from most to least and vice versa

The concept of order involves understanding that things can be placed in a row according to a pattern that goes from the least to the most and vice versa. Many logical and mathematical operations are based on this concept, such as placing blocks next to each other so as to form a staircase and counting from 1 to 10. From time to time, play some ordering games with your child.

Can you order the measuring cups from smallest to biggest?

Can you order these blocks from shortest to tallest to make a staircase?

Can you draw your family in a row?

Can you order these glasses from most to least full?

Can you put the cards in a row from 1 to 10?

Nearer, Nearer

the concept of distance

Directions

1. Select "It." He leaves the room.

2. Hide an object. Call "It" back into the room and tell him what you hid.

3. "It" walks around the room, searching for the object.

4. Give hints as "It" moves about. If he is moving nearer to the object, say, "nearer, nearer." If he starts to move away from the object, say, "farther, farther." When he is very near, say, "there!" and let him find it.

Distance words:

HERE, THERE

NEAR, NEARER, NEAREST

FAR, FARTHER, FARTHEST

Chapter 5
Sorting and Classifying

Going by various names in various books, such as *grouping, categorizing* and *making sets,* classifying is the important logical skill of sorting a collection of various things into smaller groups. The smaller groups can be based on one or more common factors, such as size, shape, function, color and origin, depending on the particular reason for sorting. Classifications are a part of our lives. Large stores sort their merchandise into departments where people can easily find what they are looking for; mothers sort laundry into various drawers and closets for the same reason. Knowing how to organize makes life easier.

In order to learn this important skill, a child must learn the concept of *sameness* and *difference,* a basic understanding that is covered in several chapters of this book. For example, in the first chapter, the words *same* and *different* come up in order to compare various sensations. In the chapter preceding this one, *same* and *different* appear again, this time so the child can use them to compare and order different sizes, amounts and weights.

In this chapter *same* things belong together in groups. Children learn to answer the questions, "Which one belongs to this group?" and "Which one doesn't belong?" A child learns to separate animal pictures and food cards. He helps his mother with the sorting tasks of everyday life: putting away laundry, groceries and his toys.

Once a child has a basic understanding of classification, he can go on to more advanced skills, such as being able to subcategorize. He can start with foods, work down to vegetables, down further to red vegetables and finally end up with a group of red vegetables that he likes to eat.

He can learn to classify together different forms of the same thing. For example, he can see the relationship between prunes in a box, stewed prunes, prune juice, prune pudding and prune pie. He understands that their common factor is their common substance: prune.

Another kind of classification skill is the ability to put together different visual representations of the same thing. Under the classification *rooster*, for example, goes a color photograph of a rooster, a black single-line outline of a rooster, a drawing of many roosters, a statue of a rooster and a toy stuffed rooster that belongs to Baby. Each of these is a different rendering, but since they are all representations of the same animal, they can be classified together.

Besides being logical, classification skills have a creative side to offer. A child who can hold up an object and think of several ways in which it could be classified has learned about flexible thinking and the important notion that there is more than one way to look at something.

Activity Chart / Sorting and Classifying

Activity	What It Teaches
which pile?	sorting and classifying on the basis of function, ownership, storage place and color
same and different games	classifying same things together; distinguishing an object that doesn't belong; realizing that you can make your own learning materials
nuts and bolts	sorting and classifying on the basis of size, shape and texture; separating a mixed pile into separate classes of things
store riddles	understanding the classification system used by stores; learning that there is more than one way to look at something
kitchen classifications	sorting and classifying on the basis of size, shape and function
pantry party	sorting and classifying on the basis of function and storage place
how to make food cards	identifying foods in many categories; realizing that materials for play can be home-made; classifying together different forms of the same thing
games with food cards:	
1. odd card	recognizing an object that does not belong in the same category as the others
2. farmer's truck	selecting objects belonging to the same given category
3. post the menu	selecting only those foods that belong in the category of one meal; selecting the pictorial representation of a real thing
animal pictures	classifying together different representations of the same thing; subcategorizing
operation toys	classifying same things together; separating a mixed pile into separate classes of things that belong together

Which Pile?

a laundry day experience in sorting skills

Materials
unsorted clean clothes

Activity
Show your child the separate piles you make when you sort laundry: Mom's pile, Kathy's pile, the towel pile, the needs-to-be-ironed pile—whatever piles you normally use. Make the sorting task into a game. Take one thing at a time and hold it up for your child to recognize and determine as to which pile it goes in.

HINT: Children love jokes they can understand and correct. For example, you might hold up a small sock and say, "Here's Daddy's sock!" Let your child set you straight.

Variations
1. Dark and Light: Your child can help you sort dirty laundry into light loads and dark loads.
2. Sorting Socks: Give your child a bunch of loose socks to sort and pair. The trick here is to match size, color and pattern.

Same and Different Games

with carbon paper

Materials
white paper
carbon paper
ballpoint pen

Instructions
1. Put a piece of carbon paper between two sheets of white paper.
2. Draw a picture of anything on the top sheet. Make sure the inky side of the carbon paper is face down.
3. Remove the carbon. You will have two identical pictures. Make more to use in the games illustrated below.

GAME 1
Find 2 pictures that are the SAME.

GAME 2
Find the picture that is different.

Nuts and Bolts

a hardware sorting game

Materials

a large jar with a wide opening, an egg carton, four to five each of twelve different things, obtainable from the hardware store: ½-inch screws, 1-inch screws, 1½-inch screws, small nuts, larger nuts, small bolts, larger bolts, small metal washers, medium metal washers, large metal washers, plastic washers, and rubber washers

How to play

Fill the jar with all the objects. The game is to sort them into the twelve compartments of the egg carton.

Variation

Use tiny objects found around the house—bobby pins, toothpicks, paper clips, buttons, coins, safety pins, cut up plastic straws, beads and dried beans.

Store Riddles

where do I go?

Knowing where to buy things involves classification. Try the following riddles on your child as you take him with you to the department store or shopping center.

Hint: A riddle may have more than one answer. Encourage your child to think of all the possibilities. For example, you can buy toys at the toy store, the 5¢ & 10¢ store and sometimes at the grocery store too.

I need eggs.
Where do I go?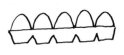

I need a toy.
Where do I go?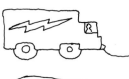

I need socks.
Where do I go?

I need a popsicle.
Where do I go?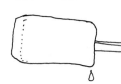

I need toothpaste.
Where do I go?

I need bread.
Where do I go?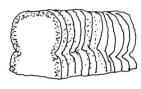

I need a hammer.
Where do I go?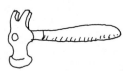

I need shoes.
Where do I go?

Kitchen Classifications

a put away game

Knives, forks and spoons

Let your child help put them away; he'll feel proud to have a chore of his own. First, make sure his hands are clean, then set the silverware down near the silverware drawer. Show him where each piece fits and then let him play and practice alone.

Plastic dishes too

If you have unbreakable dishes that are stored in a place easily accessible to your child, you might let him put them away. Soon he'll be able to classify big plates, little plates, cups, saucers and soup bowls.

Pantry Party

as you and your child store the groceries

Let your child watch and help you as you put away the groceries. Talk about the various foods and supplies and where they are kept in the kitchen.

Animal Pictures

how many different kinds can you find?

Materials
picture magazines, old cards
   and coloring books
scissors

Instructions
Cut out and save a variety of animal pictures. Look especially for different *kinds* of pictures (photographs, drawings, cartoons, silhouettes—black-and-whites as well as full-color). Your child should learn to "read" different kinds of pictorial representations.

How to use the pictures
The pictures can be sorted in many ways: into piles of different animals, into categories of animals that have four legs and those that don't, into groups that fly and those that can't fly. Help your child think of other ways to sort his pictures . . . how about separating the black-and-whites from the color pictures?

How to Make Food Cards

a do-it-yourself activity

Materials

index cards, 3-inch by 5-inch

magazines that contain pictures of food—housekeeping magazines are good

paste, glue or tape

scissors

black crayon or pen

shoe box (optional)

Instructions

1. Cut out magazine pictures of all kinds of food: meat, fish, soup, vegetables, bread, desserts and beverages. Look for different forms of the same food: mashed potatoes, canned potatoes, potato soup, french fries.
2. Paste the pictures on index cards, one picture per card.
3. Label each card (print) as your child names it.
4. Optional: Decorate a shoebox with food pictures for storage of the cards.

Hint: On your next trip to the supermarket, let your child bring along a food-card shopping list. He can help you look for the items you need.

Variation

Use two copies of the same magazine to collect identical pictures. These cards will be perfect for matching games.

TOMATO SOUP!

Games with Food Cards

use the cards you made yourselves

1. ODD CARD

APPLE	PEAR	BANANA	CARROTS

Choose a category but don't tell it. Any food category will do: vegetables, fruits or meat. Put three cards that fit your category, picture-side up, on the table. Add one more card that doesn't fit. Ask, "Which one is different?" When your child guesses the answer, ask him to replace it with a card that goes with the others.

2. FARMER'S TRUCK

You be the grocery man, your child can be the farmer. The game consists of your calling the farmer for a specific order and his delivering the order in his toy truck. If you order "only fruit," he drives a truckful of fruit cards over to you. To help him learn classification, place orders for general categories such as meat or soups.

3. POST THE MENU

While you're cooking dinner, your child finds cards that correspond with your menu. He can post them on the refrigerator door (using magnetic clips) or on a nearby window sill for everyone to see.

TOMATO SOUP
POT ROAST
POTATOES
CAKE

Operation Toys

picking up toys can be fun

Here's the way to do it: Give your child some plain white or brown shopping bags. Explain that each bag is for certain toys. One bag may be for blocks, another for doll clothes and so forth. He can color pictures of the toys on the outside of the bags, you can label them. When it is time for Operation Toys, give the child the bags, and let him put away his toys by sorting them.

Chapter 6

Counting and Measuring

Some young children learn to count without knowing what the numbers mean. They don't understand that the number 3 stands for "3 of something"—whether it be 3 grapes, 3 tugboats or 3 grandmothers. A child who doesn't understand that numbers are based on real things will have a difficult time learning arithmetic. On the other hand, a child who knows that numbers represent actual objects has a solid foundation for going on to addition, subtraction, multiplication and division.

As a parent you can help children develop number concepts in a variety of ways. You can share everyday number experiences:

When you make the laundry list, your child can help by counting the shirts.

When you go to the store, your child can get two quarts of milk from the case.

When you pay, your child can count the change or count the pennies.

When you get in line at the supermarket, your child can count the things in your basket to find out which line you belong in.

When it's time to set the table for dinner, your child can figure out how many spoons you need.

Just keep in mind that, whenever you count, you should do it in terms of something. Count beans, count spools, count money, count books or count giant steps. In this way, you'll help your child understand that numbers represent amounts. When he counts, he'll know what he's talking about.

Activity Chart / Counting and Measuring

Activity	What it Teaches
tips	suggestions for parents about making numbers meaningful
bring me five	counting things, associating numbers with corresponding groups of real things
giant steps	counting things, associating numbers with corresponding groups of real things
inventory	counting things, using number symbols to represent a group of real things
button toss	counting a group of real things
ring toss	counting things, associating numbers with corresponding groups of real things
play store	using numbers, counting things
measure up	
1. with a yardstick	comparing lengths, understanding the concept of measuring, recognizing and reading numbers, comparing numbers
2. with your feet	
see how many	associating a number with a given quantity of real things
check the time	recognizing and identifying numbers, understanding how numbers are used
more numbers	
1. how cold?	recognizing and identifying numbers, associating numbers with temperature
2. what's today?	identifying and recognizing numbers, understanding how numbers are used on a calendar
3. missing number	identifying a number by recognizing sequence

go	counting things, using numbers in a meaningful way, recognizing the comparative value of numbers
number cards	
1. order	ordering numbers, recognizing and identifying numbers
2. mystery number	recognizing and naming numbers
3. match pairs	recognizing and matching numbers that are the same
4. adding and sub-tracting	joining groups of things to make a larger group, taking away groups of things to leave a smaller group
5. number card bingo	matching numbers
number strips	
1. experiment	comparing numbers
2. what's the same?	identifying groups that are the same, recognizing number combinations that are the same
3. what can you add?	identifying and recognizing equivalence, understanding what makes groups equal
flannel board	
1. number stories	associating groups of things with corresponding numeral
2. show me	identifying and naming numerals that correspond to a group of things
3. adding ducks	joining groups of things
counting carton	associating numbers with real things, counting things
measure plus mix equals cookies	counting things, using numbers to measure

Tips

for helping your child learn to count

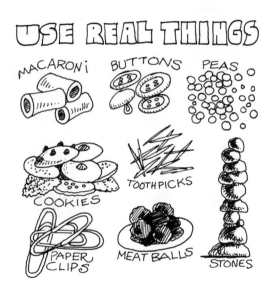

USE REAL THINGS

MACARONI BUTTONS PEAS

COOKIES TOOTHPICKS

PAPER CLIPS MEAT BALLS STONES

Touch each thing as you count it. Say, "Let's count the spoons to find out how many there are. One (touch it), two (as you touch the second), three (as you touch the third). There are four spoons. Why don't you count them?"

ONE...

Have all the things you are going to count in front of you, in other words, don't start by trying to count the houses you pass while riding in a car.

Every so often, mix up the order of things you are counting so that your child won't think that a particular thing has a particular number.

Count different things.

Count the buttons on your coat

Count the windows in the living room

Count the chairs in the kitchen

Count pennies

Count your french fries

Count your toys

Count the things on the table

Variety is important.

Don't rush. Don't push. If your child doesn't seem interested—forget it. He'll let you know when he's ready to learn.

Bring Me Five

count and count again

Activity

Say, "Please bring me five flowers." When your child brings them, put them where you both can see and count them: "1, 2, 3, 4, 5. Five flowers. Thank you."

106

Giant Steps

counting practice and good exercise

Activity

Say, "Let's play Giant Steps. First I'll tell you whether you may take giant steps or baby steps and then I will tell you how many steps you can take. After you take your steps, it will be your turn to tell me."

Say, "You may take three giant steps: 1, 2, 3." (Count along out loud as he takes them. Be sure he counts aloud as you take your steps.)

Hint: Don't forget that an occasional "mistake" on your part—as you take one step too many or leave out a number when counting—can liven up the game.

Inventory

find out how many

ITEM	NUMBER
DOGS	1
COUCHES	2
LAMPS	14
SHOES	18
DOLLS	7
SOCKS	56
CHAIRS	16
BATHTUBS	1
TELEVISIONS	2
TELEPHONES	2

Materials

pencil and paper

Activity

Together, take an inventory of things in the house. Keep a written record of the results. Count everything! How many chairs? Sofas? TV's? Tables? Cans of soup? Windows? How many socks do you have? How many socks does Daddy have? Shirts? Coats? Shoes? Toy trucks?

Variation:
A Personal Inventory

Help your child make a list of the things he can do and count how many times he can do them. Ask, "How many times can you hop on the right foot?" "Hop on your left foot?" "Jump up and down?" "Clap your hands?" "Snap your fingers?" "Jump rope without missing?"

Button Toss

it's the buttons in the bag that count

Materials

a large supply of buttons (anywhere from 5 to 20)

a paper bag (grocery size is good to start)

a yardstick or adhesive tape (or whatever is best to make a line on your floor to stand behind)

Activity

Fold down the top of a paper bag and place it on the floor. (A book in the bottom of the bag will keep it from toppling over.) Make a line on the floor a reasonable distance from the bag. You'll have to experiment to find the right distance. Say, "Stand behind this line. Throw one button at a time. See how many you can get in the bag." When all the buttons have been thrown, count the number of buttons in the bag. That's your score. Then gather up all the buttons and try again.

HINT : Practice makes perfect. And practicing means counting to find out "HOW MANY" over and over again.

Ring Toss

who has the highest number?

Materials
ten clothespins
a shallow cardboard box
five rubber jar rings

Instructions
1. Turn the box over and cut ten holes.
2. Number the holes from 1–10.
3. Stick a clothespin in each hole.

Activity
The player stands about three or four feet from the box and throws the rings, one at a time, trying to get each one over a clothespin. When a ring goes over a pin, the number by the pin hole is the score. Each player adds up his score when his turn is over. The highest score wins.

Play Store

how much? how many?

Help your child play store. Collect and price the merchandise (cookies, toys, books, old magazines, crayons, pictures). Make lots of paper money. Find buttons or bottle caps for small change. A muffin tin makes a good cash register.

Take turns buying
and selling.

Measure Up

how long? how far? how high?

1. With a Yardstick

Materials
yardstick
adhesive tape

Activity
Cover the numbers on a yardstick with adhesive tape when you first introduce your preschooler to the idea of measuring. Start by asking him to find out whether things are longer or shorter than the stick. Show him how to line the stick up with what he wants to measure. It's important to help him discover that a change in position doesn't mean a change in length. Measure everything:

How long is: the dog? your leg? Daddy's leg? the table leg? your arm? your foot? your bed? the baby?

How wide is: the refrigerator? the door? the window?

After he's caught on to how to use the yardstick, you can remove the tape and help him make more accurate measurements.

2. With Your Feet

Materials
paper
crayon
scissors

Instructions
Trace your child's foot and show him how to use it as a pattern to make lots of feet. Help him put them end-to-end to measure. Ask, "How many of your feet is it from the refrigerator to the table?" "Around the table?"

See How Many

on your number poster

Materials
large sheet of paper
glue or paste
ruler
crayons or felt-tip marker
small objects to count: O-shaped cereal, buttons
  beads, peas or beans

Instructions
The fun is in the making. Let your child play the major role.
1. Divide the paper into eleven rows.
2. In the top row write the title: Number Poster.
3. Number the remaining rows down the left side from 1–10.
4. Glue or paste the appropriate number of objects in a line beside each number. Arrange them so that it is easy for your child to see that each successive number stands for one more.

Poster Game
Point to numbers in the newspaper. Ask your child to point to the matching number on the poster.

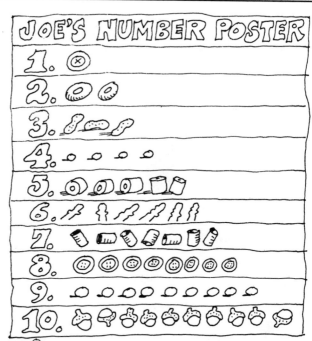

JOE'S NUMBER POSTER
1.
2.
3.
4.
5.
6.
7.
8.
9.
10.

Hint: Pop beads are wonderful for counting and comparing!

Check the Time

telling time is another chance to use numbers

I'M LATE, I'M LATE!

Telling time is one of the hardest things a child has to learn. You can help by "talking" time.

Say, "You have 10 minutes to play. At 9 o'clock you have to go to bed. When the big hand gets to 12 and the little hand is on 9 it will be 9 o'clock."

Say, "The store closes at 5 o'clock. I only have 45 minutes to get there."

Give your child a clock he can experiment with—an old broken clock or one that you and he make. Set his clock to read a time that's important to him—maybe the time a favorite TV program comes on. Say, "The hands on your clock say 7:30. When the hands on the real clock are the same as the hands on your clock, you'll know that it's 7:30 and time for your television program."

Use the electric timer on the stove. Show him how it is set. Explain that each section stands for a minute. Help him set it when there are only 15 minutes left to play before a nap. Set it just to find out how long 15 minutes is.

(For more telling time activities, see Chapter 4, page 78.)

More Numbers

1, 2, 3, 4, 5, 6, 7, 8, 9, 10

1. How Cold

"Do I have to wear my mittens?"

Hang a big outdoor thermometer where your child can see it. Make a chart for him to follow so that by reading the thermometer and reading the chart, he can answer his own question.

WHAT TO WEAR

2. What's Today?

A big piece of paper is all you need to make a special wall calendar for your child. At the beginning of the month, mark off important days coming up— such as birthdays and holidays. Write in his dentist appointment or the day Grandmother will visit. Each morning, cross off the day before and look to see what's happening and what's ahead.

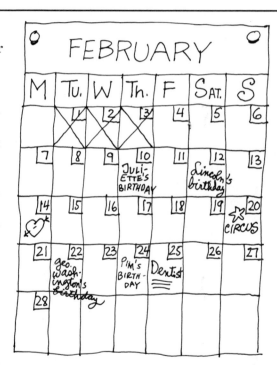

3. Missing Number

While you're waiting or traveling, say, "Listen very carefully while I count to ten. When I get through, tell me if I was right. If I left out a number, tell me what the number was."

113

Go

a counting game you can make yourself

Materials

cardboard or heavy paper
crayons
buttons or bottle caps
pair of dice

Variation

If no dice are handy, write the
numbers from 1–10 on pieces
of paper and have children
draw them from a box.

Instructions

Pick a favorite place. Then make a game that's a race to get there. Here's
how:

1.   Draw two circles on the cardboard. They can be any place you want
them. In one circle write the word *GO*. In the other circle write the name
of the place your child picked.

2.   Draw a course that goes from one circle to the other. It can be a
straight course or a winding course. It can be complex or simple. It's up
to you and your child.

3.   Divide the course into equal spaces. In some of the spaces write
directions that you and your child make up, such as:

  Miss Next Turn   Go Back 2 Spaces   Advance 3 Spaces

4.   Use bottle caps, buttons, toy racing cars or anything you have handy.

5.   Roll the dice. They determine how many spaces each player moves.

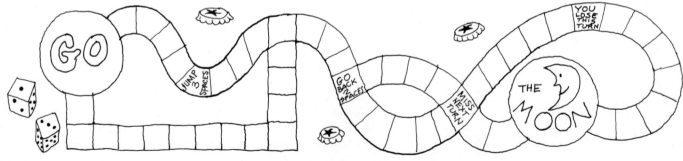

114

Number Cards

how many different ways can you arrange three things?

Materials

unlined index cards (5-inch by 8-inch is a good size)

buttons (small) and needle with heavy thread or large snaps and a paper-puncher

Instructions

Make several sets of number cards for the numbers from 1–10 by sewing the appropriate number of buttons (or snaps) on each card. No two cards for the same number should have the same arrangement of buttons. For example, the cards for the number three might look like this:

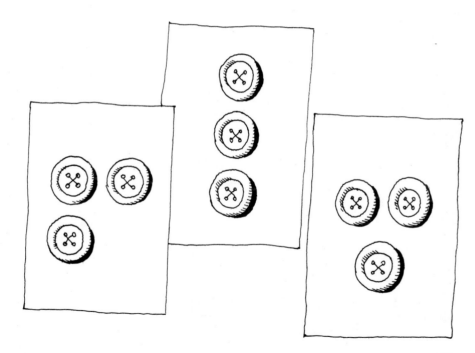

Games With Number Cards

1. ORDER

Place one set of cards on a table or on the floor. Be sure that they are not in order. Ask, "Can you put them in order?"

2. MISSING NUMBERS

Place one set of cards on the table or on the floor. Ask your child to close his eyes while you hide one of the cards. When he opens his eyes, ask, "Can you figure out which card I have?"

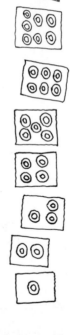

3. MATCH PAIRS

Place both sets of cards on the table or on the floor. Point to one card and ask, "Can you find another card that has the same number of buttons to match this one?"

4. ADDING AND SUBTRACTING

Take one card. Say, "Now I have three buttons." Point to a 2 card and say, "Now I'm going to take two more buttons. How many buttons do I have all together? Count them. Five buttons. Three buttons and two more buttons make five buttons all together."

Take another card. Say, "I have two buttons. I need four buttons. Can you find a card to give me so that I will have four buttons?"

Give your child a card with one button.

Ask, "What card do you need to take so that you will have the same number of buttons that I have?"

5. NUMBER CARD BINGO

6	9	3
8	5	7

Make a Bingo sheet for each player. Divide a large piece of paper into six equal sections. Each section should be as big or bigger than the number card. Write a number from 1–10 in each section. The numbers don't have to be in order. Make each Bingo sheet different. Put the number cards in a shoe box or a paper bag. The players take turns drawing a card. If a player draws a number card that matches one of his Bingo sheet numbers, he can use the card to cover the number. If not, he must put the card back in the box and wait for his next turn. The first player to cover all the numbers on his Bingo sheet wins.

Number Strips

to compare

Materials

heavy paper (one 9-inch by
   12-inch sheet)
felt-tip markers or crayons
ruler
scissors

Instructions

1. With a ruler, divide the paper into nine
   1-inch wide strips.
2. Divide each strip into twelve 1-inch squares.
3. Color and cut the strips as follows:

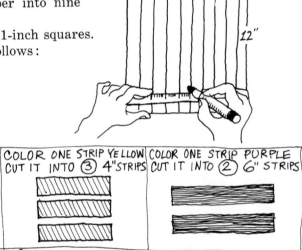

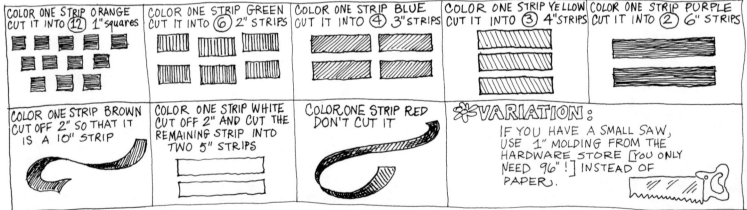

COLOR ONE STRIP ORANGE
CUT IT INTO (12) 1" squares

COLOR ONE STRIP GREEN
CUT IT INTO (6) 2" STRIPS

COLOR ONE STRIP BLUE
CUT IT INTO (4) 3" STRIPS

COLOR ONE STRIP YELLOW
CUT IT INTO (3) 4" STRIPS

COLOR ONE STRIP PURPLE
CUT IT INTO (2) 6" STRIPS

COLOR ONE STRIP BROWN
CUT OFF 2" SO THAT IT
IS A 10" STRIP

COLOR ONE STRIP WHITE
CUT OFF 2" AND CUT THE
REMAINING STRIP INTO
TWO 5" STRIPS

COLOR ONE STRIP RED
DON'T CUT IT

✿VARIATION:
IF YOU HAVE A SMALL SAW,
USE 1" MOLDING FROM THE
HARDWARE STORE [YOU ONLY
NEED 96"!] INSTEAD OF
PAPER.

Games with Number Strips

to find out about numbers

1.EXPERIMENT...PLAY

Let your child just enjoy playing with the strips. He'll soon be making his own comparisons and experimenting with combinations and patterns.

2.WHAT'S THE SAME?

Ask questions. Point to the brown strip. Ask, "What can you find that's the same length as the brown strip?" "Two white strips?" "Ten orange strips?" "What else?"

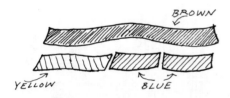

3.WHAT CAN YOU ADD?

Put the brown strip alongside the red strip. Ask, "What can you add to the brown strip to make it the same as the red strip?"

Flannel Board

anything cut out of felt will stick to it

Materials
cardboard or plywood (1½-inch by 2-inch is
  adequate)
piece of flannel (a dark color is best)
good supply of medium-weight sandpaper
thumbtacks or glue

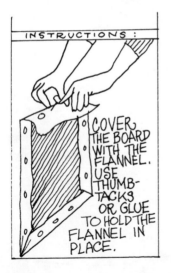

INSTRUCTIONS:

COVER THE BOARD WITH THE FLANNEL. USE THUMB-TACKS OR GLUE TO HOLD THE FLANNEL IN PLACE.

CUT NUMBERS, LETTERS, FIGURES, ANIMALS, PEOPLE, OUT OF FELT.

IF YOU DON'T HAVE ANY FELT, A SMALL PIECE OF SAND-PAPER GLUED TO THE BACK OF A PICTURE OR CUTOUT WILL MAKE IT "STICK" TO THE FLANNEL BOARD.

Activities
1. Number Stories
A simple story can become a learning event when
it's illustrated on a Flannel Board.

What to say	*What to do*
Once there was a duck who lived happily all by himself until one day . . .	Stick one duck on the Flannel Board.

What to say
Two more ducks came along. Then how many were there?

What to do
Add two more ducks on the Flannel Board.

THREE DUCKS!

2. Show Me

One person puts a number on the Flannel Board and says, "Show me." The other person "shows" by putting up that number of things on the Board.

3. Adding Ducks

Put two ducks on the Flannel Board. Put the number 2 above the group. Add two more ducks to the Flannel Board. Put the number 2 above the new group. Say, "Two ducks and two ducks means how many ducks?" Leave all the ducks, but remove the numbers 2 and 2 and replace them with the number 4. Say, "Four ducks."

Use the same method to introduce subtraction.

Counting Carton

an empty egg carton can become a learning toy

Materials
egg carton
crayons

Instructions
1. Remove the top from the egg carton.
2. Number the sections of the carton from 1–12.

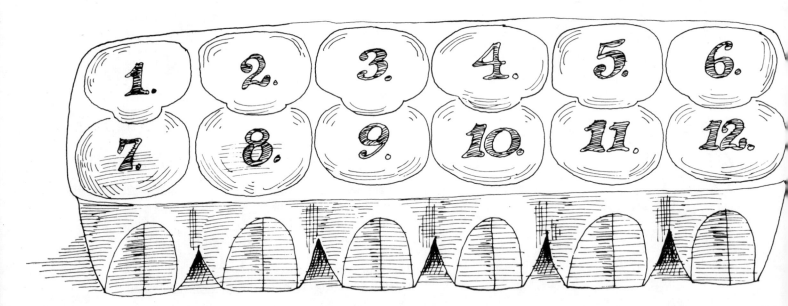

Activity

Give your child things like beans, paper clips, buttons, beads, peas, M & M's, and macaroni to put in the counting carton.

Point to the numeral 1 and say, "This says 1, so I'll put one pea in this section." (Place one pea in the 1 cup.) Point to the next cup and say, "This section says 2, so I'll put in two peas. 1, 2." You might start by letting him help you fill the sections. As soon as he catches on, he'll have fun doing it on his own. You can keep up his interest by providing new things for him to count from time to time.

Hint: If you give him exactly the right number of things (78), he'll know when he's filled each section with the right number, because there will be just enough things to fill each section, but none left over. It's a self-correcting counting game!

Measure Plus Mix Equals Cookies

count before you bake, count before you eat, count after you eat

Activity
Making cookies is a wonderful chance to use measuring and counting. Let your youngster help as much as possible. He can measure, mix, sift. He can cut out cookies with cookie cutters. (How about making some triangles, circles and squares?) He can name the shapes. He can put them on the cookie sheet. He can count how many he made. He can count how many he eats!

Variation
If making cookies from scratch isn't possible, try the refrigerator cookies available in a roll at the supermarket.

Hint: Use raisins and nuts for decoration. Count them as you put them on. Make a 3 cookie, a 4 cookie, and so on. How many nuts make a face? Two for eyes, plus one for a nose, plus five more for a smiling mouth.

124

Chapter 7

Problem Solving

> Intelligence is not how much we know how to do,
> but how we behave when we don't know what to do.
> —John Holt, *How Children Fail*

Problem-solving ability is no less than a style of life—a style so important for rational existence that children deserve to learn it when they are young. What happens when we encounter a problem? Any problem. A chair may be in the way, a person may be unhappy, a dish may have smashed into a million pieces; the question is: What are we going to do about it?

. First of all, we need to figure out what the problem is. Identifying problems is a skill, one that children do not learn without help. For example, think of a child having trouble putting on his sneakers. He may not realize that the problem is the result of tightly tied laces. Once he identifies the trouble, he can proceed to the next skill, that of figuring out one or more possible solutions. In the case of the sneakers, for example, two solutions are plausible: He can either untie the laces himself or find someone else to do it for him.

The next step in the problem-solving process is to choose a solution, hopefully the best one, and act on it. This step takes courage. Some children are so afraid of being wrong that they cannot solve problems. Their fear is usually the result of parents who insist on correct behavior. Other children develop self-confidence and are willing to take risks. Predictably, they come from homes in which the parents encourage individual thought and the notion of following through on a decision.

An important aspect of problem solving is understanding the laws of cause and effect. If you push a lamp off a table, it will fall to the floor. If you rub a crayon along the wallpaper, it will leave a mark. Once a child understands the relationship between cause and effect, he will have an intellectual foundation for learning two additional skills: (1) being able to predict what is *going* to happen in certain situations, and (2) being able to figure out what has *already* happened in others. For example, if he sees someone pushing on the lamp, he guesses that it will fall. If he sees crayon marks on the wall, he surmises how they got there.

The ability to cope with problems by identifying them and solving them does not come easily for children, nor for many adults. It takes constant practice and a sense of humor too. After all, problems do seem to be a human condition and children need to learn not to be overwhelmed by them but, instead, how to think for themselves realistically and intelligently.

Activity Chart / Problem Solving

Activity	What It Teaches
what's wrong here?	identifying problems, explaining solutions
what's missing?	identifying problems, observing details, remembering details
patterns	perceiving patterns, predicting patterns, imitating patterns, following visual directions
accidents will happen	understanding the laws of cause and effect, anticipating future events
talking about problems	identifying problems, discussing causes, figuring out solutions, acting on solutions
what if?	understanding the laws of cause and effect, anticipating future events

What's Wrong Here?

a game for identifying problems

In this game the parent purposely makes obvious mistakes for the child to discover and correct. For each mistake the parent asks, "What's wrong here?" As you discuss the problem with your child, encourage complete answers as illustrated. Some "mistakes" to make:

Try to eat a banana without peeling the skin off.

Try to pour milk out of an unopened carton.

Try to put on your shoe when it is laced and tied.

Try to put on a shirt without unbuttoning it.

Try to pour soup out of an unopened can.

Try to eat with an upside-down spoon.

Try to sit on a chair that is turned on its side.

Try to brush your hair with the wrong end of the hairbrush.

What's Missing?

a game for would-be detectives

1. Parent and child look at objects on the table.

2. Parent holds up a cardboard screen while he removes one object.

3. The child tries to guess which object is missing.

What's Missing? is a problem-solving game that develops observation skills and memory. You can make this game very simple or quite hard depending on the ability of your child. At first, start out with only a few objects. When your child can successfully name the missing object several times in a row, add a few more objects or change them altogether. Reverse the roles occasionally: Let your child hide an object while you try to guess. Suggested objects for this game are:

knife, fork, spoon, large spoon, spatula, can opener

many crayons, each of a different color

the letters of the alphabet, each written on a separate slip of paper

several pictures, cut from magazines

several playing cards, each a different suit and number

an assortment of small toys

Patterns

what comes next?

Materials
colored plastic toothpicks

Procedure
With your child watching, lay out the toothpicks according to a set pattern. The design you make should consist of a regular color pattern repeated over and over.

As you lay down the toothpicks, help your child perceive the pattern. After you think he has caught on, ask him, "What comes next?" See if he can select the correct color toothpick and place it according to the pattern.

Variation
Copy Cat
Lay out a toothpick pattern for your child to copy with his own set of toothpicks.

Hint: If your child doesn't seem interested in playing the above games, let him play with the toothpicks however he wants. Don't *force* a child to play according to your rules.

WHAT COMES NEXT?

Accidents Will Happen

you can use them for learning

Until a child sees what happens when a fresh egg is dropped on the kitchen floor, he will not understand why eggs must be carried very carefully. Children learn from accidents—how they happened, what the result was, and how to prevent future ones. Take the time to talk about accidents with your child.

HOW DID THE PLANT GET KNOCKED OVER?

WHAT HAPPENS IF YOU LEAVE THE WATER ON IN THE TUB?

WHAT HAPPENS WHEN YOU COOK PEAS TOO MUCH?

WHY DID THE EGG BREAK?

HOW DID THE ICE CREAM CONE FALL ON THE GROUND?

Talking About Problems

as they come up every day

3 KEY QUESTIONS

1. What is the Problem?

2. What caused the Problem?

3. How can we make it better?

If you want your child to learn problem-solving skills and attitudes, you must take the time to talk about problems as they occur. This is not always easy to do. Problems occur at unexpected moments, often the worst moments. Nevertheless, if you can, take a minute to discuss them with your child. Use the questions on the left. Analyze several solutions and decide which one is best. Act on it. Show by your example that problems can be solved.

If the problem is such that it is impossible to discuss at the moment of occurrence, save it for later, perhaps dinner, when the rest of the family can talk about it with you.

The kinds of problems that arise

Problems come in all sizes and shapes . . . some big, some small, some long-lasting and others short-lived. Teach your child that problems of all kinds are a part of everyday life, and that it is best not to fear them but to know how to deal with them.

In addition to minor household catastrophes, such as spilled milk, children are often faced with problems caused by bad weather. Rain means that they can't go out. What to do? Help them realize that, since they can't change the weather, the answer is to think up something especially fun to play inside.

Many problems are emotional ones. A child may not want to share his toys. He may be angry because he feels left out. Whatever the trouble is, it is more likely to be appeased by talking about it. Use the three key questions. What is the matter? Why do you feel this way? What can *we* do to make you feel better?

What If?

a game of cause and effect

What If? helps children learn to anticipate results. To play, set up a situation like the ones listed below. Pose your question, giving the child time to guess the outcome before it occurs.

What will happen to the milk if we add chocolate syrup to it?

What will happen to red paint if we mix it with yellow?

What will happen to the ice cream if we put it in a hot oven?

What will happen to the water if we add bubble bath?

What will happen to a balloon if we poke it with a pin?

What will happen to a dish of water left out for a week?

Try some questions that spur the imagination.

What if the sun stopped shining?

What if animals could talk like people?

WHAT WILL HAPPEN IF I ADD A DROP OF RED FOOD COLORING?

Chapter 8

Exploring

Experimenting is a way of playing, a way of finding out what something is all about. A young child concentrating on how certain objects float is much like an advanced scientist discovering a new principle. The joy of exploration, of discovery, of awe is the same on any level.

There's a knack to making exploring fun. The parent's role is a delicate one and one that changes from situation to situation. When a child is busy discovering, he doesn't need or want a parent to tell him the answer or show him how something works. He wants to find out for himself. Often the parent must hold himself back and resist his temptation to interfere. Sometimes the parent's role may be that of planner—planning ways his child can be left to experiment and explore on his own. For example, children love to experiment with water. It's up to the parent to find the right place and the right clothes and to establish guidelines so that the child can be free to explore. It's up to the parent to be ready with the right tools: When a child begins to tire of playing with boats, the prepared parent is ready with funnels and pitchers.

At other times, the parent's role may be more active—it may be that of co-explorer. When your child asks, "Where does the rain come from?" part of your answer may be a simple experiment. Put some water in a saucer.

Set the saucer on a window sill where your child can check it every day. Ask, "What happened to the water?" Maybe you can follow up the experiment at bathtime by pointing out the moisture on the mirror. Ask, "Where did the water come from? Could it be the same water that disappeared from the saucer?"

While the parent's role is a changing one, it is nonetheless an important one. Be ready to share things that happen every day. When you lift the lid from a steaming pot, point out the moisture inside the lid. When you have trouble unscrewing a jar lid, run hot water on it to demonstrate that heat makes metal expand. Next time you pour liquid from a can, let your child try pouring when there is only one hole punched. If you are excited by everyday wonders, your child will be, too.

Activity Chart / Exploring

Activity	What It Teaches
water, water, everywhere	developing awareness of the natural environment, discovering the natural characteristics of water, experimenting to find out, testing hypotheses
pets	developing awareness of differences and similarities of living things
look closer	discovering new aspects of familiar things, developing curiosity, making comparisons
experiments	suggestions for parents on setting up experiments
what makes them grow?	developing awareness of the natural environment, discovering how plants grow and what plants need to live, observing and comparing, drawing conclusions
where's air?	experimenting to find out, discovering the characteristics of air, observing and drawing conclusions
what's inside?	developing curiosity, exploring to find answers, discovering new aspects of familiar things
rainy day adventures	exploring and discovering the world, developing curiosity and awareness
make butter	experimenting, observing details and drawing conclusions
mudpies and sandtarts	developing awareness of the natural environment and natural materials
trips	asking questions to find answers, observing to find answers, drawing conclusions, understanding how things work, understanding how things are made
where does garbage come from?	developing an awareness of manmade materials and of our environment, questioning what one finds, experimenting to bring about change, drawing conclusions

Water, Water, Everywhere

water play with a purpose

Materials

old raincoat	sponges	soap suds
washtub	medicine dropper	funnel
sieve	empty detergent	egg beater
pitcher	bottles (plastic)	blocks
plastic tops	basters	plastic glass
balls	newspaper	straws
	squeeze bottles	

Activity

Water play is one of a preschooler's favorite activities. It also happens to be an important learning event. Your role is to supply the water, a place to play, a few rules and materials to experiment with. Bathtime is always a good place to experiment and guarantees less mess. You can also set up a water play station in the basement or in the yard. Fill a washtub halfway to the top. Place it on a table or on a floor covered with newspaper. An old raincoat cut off and turned backwards makes a wonderful waterproof smock.

HINT: When interest wanes, stir things up by adding a dash of liquid soap to the water and handing your child an egg beater.

activities with water

1. What Floats? What Sinks?
Give water play a new dimension by discussing things that float. "Which of these floats?" Try paper, plastic, sponge, soap, metal, a bottle . . . open? closed? After experimenting with a few things, let your child guess whether or not things will float before you try them.

3. Another Experiment
What happens when paper is put in water? Try it.
When aluminum is put in water? Try it.
When sugar is put in water? Try it.
(If you think it disappeared, taste it.)

4. Carry Water
How many ways can you find to carry water?

5. Water and Heat
What happens when water is heated? Put it on the stove and see. What happens when water gets cold? Put it in the freezer and see.

2. Salt Water
What will float in salt water? What will sink in salt water? Add salt to the water and test the things you tried in plain water.

Pets

they have a lot to teach us

The case for pets is convincing. They provide children with a variety of learning experiences plus the joy of possession. With this joy goes responsibility, and pets are often one of the first real responsibilities children encounter. They learn that a pet is not a toy—it is a living thing. Once they can make this distinction, they are old enough to take care of one.

Pets provide children with an opportunity to learn about the needs of animals: food, sleep, cleanliness, exercise. And when pets give birth, the event is a natural occasion for sex education.

Be sure to deal with the death of a pet directly. Answer your child's questions as completely as you can. Never flush a dead pet away. Be sure he is honored with a proper burial.

Select a pet that will adapt to your family and feel comfortable in your home. Check with your pet store operator and veterinarian for specific information about the pet you choose.

Dogs: They're wonderful. It's better to get a puppy that can grow up with your child. An older dog may seem less trouble, but he may not be used to children. If you are a city dweller, be ready to walk him three times a day. Unless you live close to a park where a big dog can get the exercise he needs, think small.

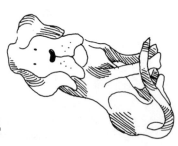

Cats: Cats are lovely and graceful. They're particularly good for small quarters. They're clean and usually house-break themselves.

Goldfish, guppies, turtles, tropical fish: Any of these makes a good pet. They're inexpensive and require less care than a dog or cat. You'll have to oversee feeding and cleaning.

Parakeets: They're playful and can be tamed. With patience and persistence many of them can be taught to talk. Be prepared to clean the cage often.

Gerbils: Known for their marvelous curiosity, gerbils make wonderful pets for children. They need little care—their cage needs to be cleaned only once every several weeks—and a day's feeding is a few tablespoons of dry birdseed and a bit of lettuce or fruit.

Anthill: Fascinating for all ages! If your pet store doesn't have one, ask the manager to order one for you.

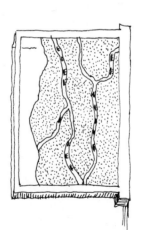

145

Look Closer

you and your child can take turns

Materials
magnifying glass

Instructions
Keep the magnifying glass handy—
where your child can find it.

You can help your child "see"
more clearly by asking questions:
"What does it look like?"
"Does it look smooth?"
"Is it moving?"

Activity
Take a closer look at the things around you:

your hand	the table	snowflakes	insects	ants
a leaf	a flower		bark	hair
a fly			plant stems	cloth
			moss	an earthworm
			grass	a spider
				a spider's web
				a drop of water

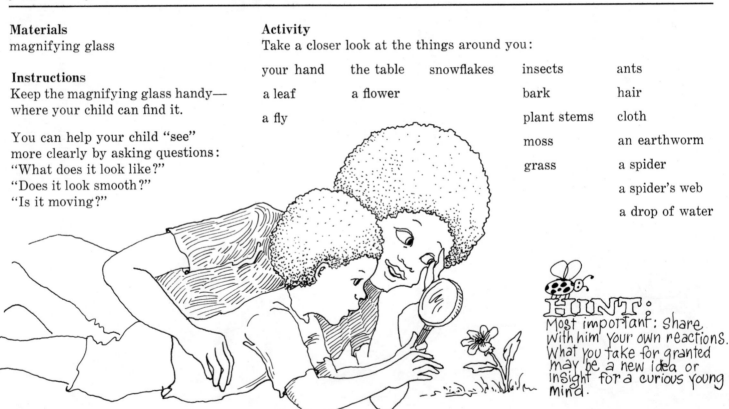

HINT:
Most important: share
with him your own reactions.
What you take for granted
may be a new idea or
insight for a curious young
mind.

146

Experiments Answer Questions

and help children learn how to find out for themselves

Let your child direct his own discoveries. This doesn't count you out by any means. You set the stage and you guide the drama by building on your child's questions.

Before: Talk about "What are we trying to find out?" "How will we find out?" "What do you think will happen?"

After: Talk about what happened. It's important to help your child put it into words. "Would it happen again if we did it again?" "What did we learn?"

Experiment to find out. Put one outside and the other on the radiator.

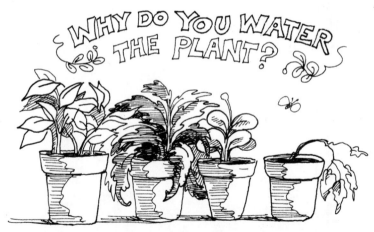

Experiment: What happens when a plant isn't watered?

What Makes Them Grow?

Plants

All the following plants can be grown indoors by young children. Teach them to test whether a plant needs water by feeling the soil. If it is damp, don't water. Only water when the soil feels dry or when the plant leaves look droopy. To demonstrate how plants need sun, put one in the shade for a week or so. What happens?

HOW TO PLANT:

WHAT TO PLANT: Lemon, Grapefruit and Orange Seeds

Poke a few small holes in the bottom of a small plastic container. Fill with soil. Insert seeds in soil. They should be covered with about ¼ inch of soil. Water. Be patient . . . it takes a while for seeds to sprout.

Avocado Pit

Use toothpicks to hold the neck of the avocado pit in the neck of a jar or glass so that the tip is in the water. Keep in a warm place out of direct sunlight. Add water from time to time to keep the tip in water. When roots have formed (it may take six weeks) and the stem has appeared, plant in soil. Don't cover the top of the seed.

Grass Seed

Sprinkle some on a damp sponge. Keep it damp and presto!

Pineapple Top

Slice off the top of a fresh pineapple and place the fruit part in a jar of water. The jar should support the foliage while the fruit part hangs in water. Roots and new leaves will grow.

Carrot Top

Remove leaves from carrot if necessary. Slice ½ inch off the top. Put in shallow dish of water and wait.

Celery Heart

Put the inside part of the celery bunch (heart and a few small leaves) in a small glass with water.

Sweet Potato

Place potato in jar with toothpicks, as described for avocado. Either end of the potato will do. After the roots have formed and the stem has appeared, plant in soil. You may be surprised to discover what a lovely delicate plant this clumsy vegetable produces.

Lima Bean

Line a glass jar with a damp paper towel. Place the lima bean between the towel and the jar so you can see it from the outside. Cover the jar. Your child will be able to watch how seeds turn into plants.

P.S.: Plants they have grown themselves make nice gifts for children to give to special people.

149

Where's Air?

some experiments to start out with

Pour Juice

Next time you open a can of liquid, punch just one hole and ask your child to pour. Why doesn't it pour evenly? What's happening? Punch a second hole. Try pouring again. What makes the difference? Air!

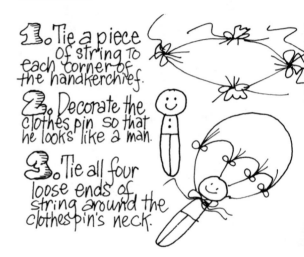

Submerge a Glass

Push a wad of paper partway inside a glass. Submerge the glass—open end first—in a pan of water. What happened to the paper? Why didn't the paper get wet? Air!

Try it again. This time tilt the glass while it's under water. What makes the bubbles? Feel the paper. What happened?

A Toy Parachute

Launch a clothespin man and watch him float back to earth on *air*.

Materials

clothespin
felt-tip markers or crayons (to decorate clothespin)
cotton handkerchief
four pieces of string —each about 12 inches long

Instructions

1. Tie a piece of string to each corner of the handkerchief.

2. Decorate the clothespin so that he looks like a man.

3. Tie all four loose ends of string around the clothespin's neck.

Activity

Ask, "What do you think will happen if we throw this up in the air?" Experiment and find out. Roll up the parachute and throw man and all as high as you can. Watch the parachute open and fill with *air!*

What's Inside?

let's look and see

Activity

Together explore the
  mysteries of:
a cabbage cut in half
an apple cut in half
a clock (if you have an
  old one)
a golf ball (try to peel off
  the outer case)
a telephone (unscrew the
  two screws on the
  bottom and the outer
  case slips off)
a mattress (maybe you'll
  see an ad in a news-
  paper or an old one on
  the street)
a flashlight
a manhole
a flower
a nut
a rubber ball
a balloon
a pencil

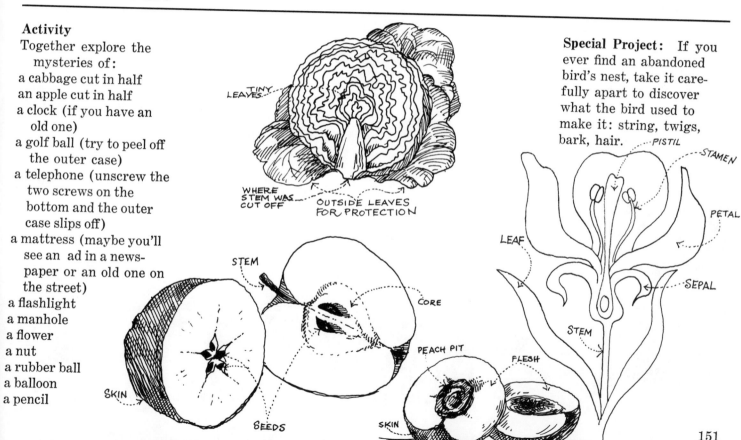

WOW!

TINY
LEAVES

WHERE
STEM WAS
CUT OFF

OUTSIDE LEAVES
FOR PROTECTION

STEM

CORE

SKIN

SEEDS

PEACH PIT

FLESH

SKIN

Special Project: If you
ever find an abandoned
bird's nest, take it carefully apart to discover
what the bird used to
make it: string, twigs,
bark, hair.

PISTIL

STAMEN

PETAL

LEAF

SEPAL

STEM

151

Rainy Day Adventures

things to keep in mind

Experiment with a Magnet
A simple horseshoe magnet will provide your child with lots of opportunities for discovery. Ask, "What can you move with the magnet?"

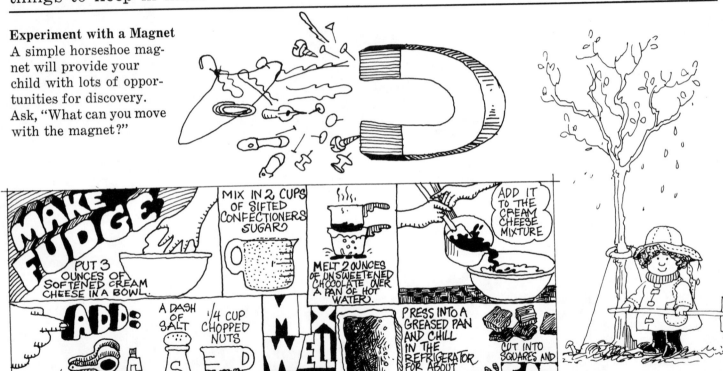

MAKE FUDGE

PUT 3 OUNCES OF SOFTENED CREAM CHEESE IN A BOWL.

MIX IN 2 CUPS OF SIFTED CONFECTIONERS SUGAR

MELT 2 OUNCES OF UNSWEETENED CHOCOLATE OVER A PAN OF HOT WATER.

ADD IT TO THE CREAM CHEESE MIXTURE

ADD:

1/4 TEASPOON VANILLA

A DASH OF SALT

1/4 CUP CHOPPED NUTS

MIX WELL

PRESS INTO A GREASED PAN AND CHILL IN THE REFRIGERATOR FOR ABOUT 15 MINUTES.

CUT INTO SQUARES AND

EAT

Plant a Tree

Get on the Nearest Bus (or subway) and ride to the last stop.

Watch a Plant Drink
Fill a glass with water and add red food coloring. Cut the bottom off a carrot, the stem of a white carnation and a stalk of celery and put all three in the glass of water. Let them stand for several hours. The carnation will change color. Cut open the carrot and the stalk of celery. What happened?

153

Make Butter

a lot of beating—a lot of drama

Materials   heavy cream (1 pint)   egg beater   large bowl   salt

1. WHAT DO YOU THINK WILL HAPPEN IF WE BEAT THIS CREAM WITH THE EGG BEATER?

GIVE YOUR CHILD A CHANCE TO SUGGEST WHAT SHE THINKS WILL HAPPEN. THEN SAY: "LET'S FIND OUT!"

2. SHOW HER HOW TO BEAT THE CREAM WITH THE EGG BEATER.

3. STOP AND TASTE WHEN YOU REACH THE WHIPPED CREAM STAGE.

4. THEN BEAT ON UNTIL FLECKS OF BUTTER APPEAR

BUTTER

5. SLOTTED SPOON

POUR OFF THE MILK. [IT'S BUTTERMILK!] AND...

BUTTER-MILK

6. MASH THE BUTTER TOGETHER INTO A BALL. TASTE. IT'S SWEET BUTTER.

7. ADD A LITTLE SALT AND TASTE AGAIN.

8. USE IT FOR DINNER. THE WHOLE FAMILY CAN HEAR WHERE IT CAME FROM, AND YOUR YOUNGSTER CAN ENJOY SHARING SOMETHING SHE MADE WITH THE WHOLE FAMILY.

154

Mudpies and Sandtarts

the joys of natural materials

Materials

old clothes or
  water smock
earth
sand
water pail
shovel
assorted molds
disposable
  cake tins

Activity

Mixing and molding just for the fun of it is a valuable activity for preschoolers. Of course, at the same time, your child is finding out a lot about water, earth and sand. Left to his own devices he will discover a lot about consistency (what happens when it's too mushy or too dry) and will learn about molding, about mixing until smooth—and about the power of the sun (why does the mud dry out?).

HINT: Supply measuring cups or measuring spoons for molds. Use the mud cakes or sand cakes to teach the words:
· BIG · BIGGER · BIGGEST.

Trips

adventure is just around the corner

A trip to the corner drugstore can become an adventure and a chance to explore when you spend a little time setting the stage. If possible, to telephone and make an appointment to visit. Take a little time to talk about where you are going, what you might see and what you'd like to find out. "What do you think you'll see?" "What do you think the firemen do when there isn't a fire?" "What do you think Daddy will be doing at his office?"

The Firehouse

What tools do firemen use? Try on a fireman's hat. Find out how firemen know where to go. What does each fireman do at the fire?

A Construction Site

Go daily to see what progress has been made. What machines do they use? Watch one man at a time. See if you can guess what his job is. Do all the workmen do the same thing?

The Post Office

Take a self-addressed letter and find out what happens when you mail it. Look for it in your mailbox the next day.

The Newspaper

How does the newspaper get the news? Who takes the pictures? Who writes the stories?

Daddy at Work

What does Daddy do all day?

The Zoo or The Pet Shop

Go at feeding time. Find out what different animals and birds eat. Find out how they eat. Do they use claws? Teeth? Beak?

A Bakery

Smell bread baking. Buy a loaf to take home. Anything else to taste or watch?

The Police Station

Ask how the two-way radio works. What does a policeman do all day?

The Local Dump

Introduce ecology. Find out where the garbage goes. What happens to it? How much garbage do you have? Think of ways to cut down.

The Library

All those books! Talk to the librarian. Ask her to show you what she does. Pick a book together. Find out how many books she's read!

The Florist

Go. Watch the florist make big arrangements for a wedding. How many different flowers can you see? How many different smells? Take a plant home.

Where Does Garbage Come From?

an introduction to ecology

Activity

Start your youngster on the right foot by calling his attention to the everyday things we all do to pollute our world. Together explore the problem and the alternatives.

Start at home. Take a look at *your* garbage. What's unnecessary? What can you do? Here are some ideas to start you and your child thinking:

Kind of Garbage	What You Can Do
All organic material: leaves, food, egg shells, coffee grounds, tea leaves	Replenish the soil—start a compost heap. Together find more information about how and where you can do it.
Bottles, aluminum cans	Return them for re-use. Together find out which ones can be returned and where you can return them. Buy those in the future.
Paper products	Stop using them when you can (paper plates and cups for example). Buy only white paper products, since dyes used to color paper products pollute our water.

What else? Together read about the subject. Help your child send away for more information. Make it a family project.

Chapter 9

Creativity

Why is it that most children love to draw, color and paint while only a few adults consider themselves talented enough to enjoy such pursuits? When a preschooler takes up a paintbrush for the first time, he never stops to consider whether or not he has "artistic ability." The very fact that he *wants* to paint leads him to an activity in which he creates a paint and paper world of his own. He paints what he feels and that's all that matters to him.

Creativity seems to be a natural, spontaneous trait in most children. Parents who want their children to be creative should concern themselves not with "teaching" it but with sustaining and nourishing the creative spirit that is already there. The best nourishment a child can get is materials to work with and respect for what he creates. Too many teachers and parents reveal their lack of respect when they teach a child *how* to draw a pumpkin and *how* to make a puppet from a commercial kit. The effect of showing a child the "right" way is negative; the result is a less creative child. The creative activities described in this book assume that your child will be encouraged to create whatever he wants.

Not all of the activities have to do with the visual arts. More than talent with a paintbrush, creativity is a way of thinking about one's environment, a way of inventing new games, a way of using a found object for a toy, a way of making someone happy. Creativity is basically an attitude, one that comes easily to young children, but must be sustained and strengthened lest it be sacrificed in our sometimes too logical world.

Activity Chart / Creativity

Activity	What It Teaches
checklist	requirements for a creative home
the pleasures of paint	how to set up for painting activities, what to do with finished paintings
crayons	two special ways to use them: (1) magic pictures, and (2) fingernail etchings
charades	how to express stories dramatically
beautiful junk	how to create sculptures out of junk found in the home and outside
think creative	how to make creative thinking a way of life
collage	how to create an abstract picture out of scraps of material
play clay	how to make play clay, ways to enjoy it

Checklist

to see if your home encourages creativity

Do you have basic art supplies?

☐ crayons   Buy fat crayons for children. Eight colors are sufficient.

☐ paint   Dry powder paint is the least expensive and easy to mix.

☐ brushes   3–4 brushes, about 1 inch wide. Short handles are best.

☐ paint clothes   Old, large shirts, smocks, plastic aprons, overalls.

☐ paper   Try newspaper, paper bags, shelf paper, old wallpaper.

☐ blunt scissors   Because they have rounded points, they are the safest for young children.

☐ paste   Buy a white paste or glue that works on cloth and paper.

Is the environment right?

☐ space   A place for your child to paint and model clay . . . in the kitchen, playroom, bedroom, bathroom or outside.

☐ storage   Use a large cardboard box, decorated with your child's artwork. Keep in an easily accessible place. Include a roll of paper towels.

☐ display   Hang paintings on the refrigerator with magnets, on a special bulletin board, on a clothesline with clothespins or in picture frames that are changed frequently.

☐ praise   Probably the single most crucial element in a creative home, you can never give enough of it.

The Pleasures of Paint

at home—with a minimum of mess

Getting started

If you're using powder paint, mix it with water in small juice cans (half full) until it is the consistency of thick soup. Use good basic colors: red, yellow, blue and perhaps one other color. Each color should have its own brush to prevent unnecessary mess. If you don't have brushes, try sponges or cotton-tipped swabs. Make sure your child has his paint clothes on and that the paint area is protected with newspapers.

Once you have taken the above precautions, relax. By all means, teach your child to be careful, but don't overdo it. If your child worries too much about tidiness, he'll not have much fun painting.

KIDS LOVE TO PAINT

Let him paint whatever he wants. It doesn't matter whether his pictures are recognizable to you. A youngster enjoys sloshing colors on paper according to his own imagination and emotion. Let him be. Encourage his creativity and hang his pictures where everyone can see them.

What to do with finished paintings

① Put up a picture gallery.

② Save them for wrapping paper.

Crayons

two special ways to use them

You will need

white or yellow crayon   paint (one color)
white paper   paintbrush

1. MAGIC PICTURES

With the crayon,
draw a scribbly
picture on the paper.
Leave a lot of the paper
clean. You now have
an almost invisible
picture.

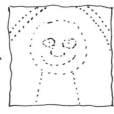

Paint the entire piece
of paper with the paint.
Suddenly the invisible
picture comes to life,
and you have a magic
picture to hang up
when dry.

2. FINGERNAIL ETCHINGS

Using all the crayons,
but the black one, cover
the paper with blotches
of color. Press down hard
as you color.

When finished, take the
black crayon and, pressing
hard, color the whole
piece of paper, covering
the other colors.

Now, with your fingernail,
scratch a picture
on the paper. The black
crayon will be removed
where you scratch,
leaving the color to
show underneath.
If fingernails are too
short, use a nail or
toothpick.

Charades

for preschool actors and actresses

Dramatic play nurtures the spirit of creativity. The next time you read a favorite story to your children, ask them to take the parts of the characters. As you read, they will act out the story—complete with costumes and props.

Try stopping at a high point so that the children can carry on with their play without a narration.

When your children have had sufficient experience, they will be able to act out stories for each other to guess, in the same manner that adults play charades.

Beautiful Junk

inside junk

Kitchen Animals

Disposable food containers can be washed and dried, then taped and tied together to form animal bodies. Use Popsicle sticks for legs.

Cities and Villages

Save various sizes of boxes and cardboard rolls for a miniature city or town. Decorate with crayons or paint. Populate with clothespin people.

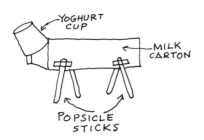

YOGHURT CUP

MILK CARTON

POPSICLE STICKS

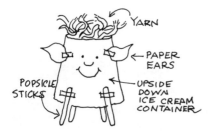

YARN

PAPER EARS

POPSICLE STICKS

UPSIDE DOWN ICE CREAM CONTAINER

Styrofoam Mobiles

Many gifts and appliances are packed in Styrofoam. Don't throw it away! Your child can paint it, cut it, poke it with colored toothpicks and hang it up as a mobile.

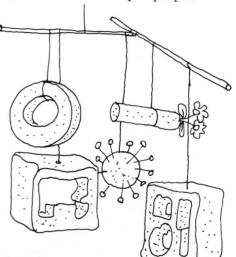

outside junk

Junk Yard Monsters

You can make monsters out of broken furniture, bleach bottles, engine parts, pipes, boards, broomsticks, hubcaps and old pails. All you need is an interesting collection of rubbish and a wild imagination.

Pile up the junk in your backyard or in a vacant lot, forming the shape of a monster. Some pieces and parts will need to be attached with string, rope or heavy-duty tape. Add facial features, bright paint and maybe an old hat. Don't forget to give the monster a name!

Think Creative

challenge your child's imagination

HOW MANY WAYS CAN YOU USE A TIN CAN?

HOW MANY WAYS CAN YOU WHISTLE?

HOW MANY WAYS CAN YOU USE OLD WRAPPING PAPER?

HOW MANY WAYS CAN YOU PLAY WITH A RUBBER BALL?

HOW MANY WAYS CAN YOU SAY "I LOVE YOU"?

HOW MANY WAYS CAN YOU LACE YOUR SHOE?

HOW MANY ANIMALS CAN YOU IMITATE?

HOW MANY THINGS CAN YOU WEAR TO PROTECT YOURSELF FROM THE RAIN?

HOW MANY WAYS CAN YOU MAKE YOUR FRIEND SMILE?

HOW MANY WAYS CAN YOU THINK OF TO EAT HOT DOGS?

HOW MANY WAYS CAN YOU WALK FROM HOME TO THE STORE?

HOW MANY WAYS CAN YOU USE A PAPER BAG?

HOW MANY WAYS CAN YOU SWING ON A SWING?

HOW MANY WAYS CAN YOU SAY "GOOD NIGHT"?

HOW MANY WAYS CAN YOU KEEP COOL IN THE SUMMER?

HOW MANY WAYS CAN YOU DRAW A TREE?

HOW MANY WAYS CAN YOU LAUGH? HO HO!

Collage

a little bit of everything and a lot of paste

Materials

paper, paste, scissors
odd scraps such as:
  string, yarn,
  cut up pieces of plastic,
  aluminum foil,
  old gum wrappers,
  cloth, ribbon, rickrack

paper clips, bobby pins,
pictures, photos,
green stamps,
feathers,
bark, leaves, sticks,
seeds, seashells,
macaroni, dried beans

Instructions

Stick the objects and scraps on the paper any way you want. If some of the materials won't stick with the paste you are using, try taping or sewing them on. When you are finished, you can protect the collage with transparent cellophane wrap. Some children, however, prefer to leave their collage uncovered so that they can feel its textures.

Variation 1: Make a collage of things found in the kitchen.

Variation 2: Make a collage out of things that remind you of a person, for example, a grandmother collage.

Play Clay

you can make it from salt, flour and water

Recipe
(Let the children help you make it!)

2 cups Flour   1 Tablespoon Salad Oil
3/4 cup Salt   1/2 cup water

Mix the water and the salad oil. Stir in the flour and the salt. Work with your hands until the mixture is smooth and thick as bread dough. If necessary, add more water.

Drops of food coloring can be added to some of the dough. As the children knead in the color, they will first see streaks of color and then, as they knead some more, a uniform color will appear.

Play clay is reusable if stored in a plastic bag in the refrigerator.

Note: Play clay is more like dough than commercial clay. Children like to push, squeeze, roll and pound it rather than model it into realistic objects. Simple things can be made, however, such as the following:

Cookies and cakes
Flatten the clay with your hands. Use a cookie cutter or a glass to cut out cookies. Cakes and cookies can be baked in make-believe ovens.

Balls and snakes
Use your hands to roll out balls and long skinny snakes. Sometimes snakes turn into string beans when cut with scissors.

Chapter 10

Self-Esteem

Much has been written for educators about the importance of each child's developing a positive image of himself. One reason for the emphasis is this: Educators have found that children who do not like themselves suffer educationally. An important aspect of self-esteem is self-confidence. Children who lack self-confidence spend so much of their energy fighting anxieties within that they have none left over for the business of learning. For such an unhappy child, a new experience is not exciting but threatening. Thinking that he will fail whatever he attempts, a child without self-confidence gives up on himself.

Fortunately, most parents love their children and show it. Nevertheless, from time to time children do suffer insecurities, whether they are caused by the presence of a new baby in the home, a move into a strange neighborhood, a divorce or whatever. Even the most devoted parent has a bad day every once in a while. At these times, parents should pay particular attention to the feelings of their children. There are many ways to show a child love. One of the most important is to share an experience with him in which he rediscovers how important he is to himself and you.

Of course, the self-esteem activities in this chapter need not be saved for bad times. On the contrary, they should be a part of a child's everyday experience. For besides building up self-confidence, another important aspect of self-esteem is learning how to express one's emotions. Happiness, sadness, anger, fear and frustration are feelings that everyone has, and it is important for a child to know that. The skill of being able to "get your feelings out" will prevent the internal turmoil that builds up when emotions, especially the angry ones, are bottled up inside.

Another point is pride. The sense of accomplishment that one feels when he has done a task or made something all by himself is a feeling that children should know at an early age. The skills of planning an activity, working on it and completing it develop the sense of responsibility and follow-through that promote the feelings of accomplishment and pride.

A child who has a sense of his own esteem delights in learning that there is no one else in the whole world who is exactly like him. Only he looks a certain way, has a certain family and neighborhood, likes and dislikes certain things. All these facts add up to his identity—a unique person with the potential for freedom and happiness.

Concurrent with a child's discovery of his own special self is the discovery that other people have selves, too. They also count. Friends, family, relatives, people on television—they all have their own personalities, own ideas, own possessions and own preferences. In this world of many people, what could be more important than the development of skills that will help children get along with others. As a parent, you are in a good position to help a child learn the skills of cooperation, negotiation and patience, as well as basic attitudes of honesty, fairness and compassion.

Activity Chart / Self-Esteem

Activity	What It Teaches
diary	developing an awareness of self and a sense of importance
self-portrait	developing an awareness of self, recognizing distinguishing characteristics
paper bag masks	recognizing and naming emotions, expressing feelings
a picture map	developing an awareness of one's neighborhood, developing an identity
mail away	developing a sense of importance and a separate identity
play kits	developing an awareness of the roles people play, understanding roles by acting them out, developing a sense of self
make a family tree	identifying the people who make a family, developing an identity, understanding the concept of family
a special vest	a feeling of pride in one's self, developing a sense of identity
blow up	developing an awareness of self and a feeling of pride
birthday parties	developing a feeling of pride and importance
a time line	developing an awareness of self and a sense of self

Diary

a day-by-day story

Materials
a large scrap book
scissors
glue or paste
crayons or felt-tip markers

Activity
Help your child keep a diary. Set aside some time after
a trip, a birthday party or any special event to record
what happened. Write the date of the event at the top
of the page and then ask, "What do you want to say
about our trip?" "What did you like best? Why did you
like it best?" Write down whatever he dictates. Illustrate the page with souvenirs or photographs from the
trip.

A diary is a good place to paste all kinds of treasures
—favorite drawings, paintings or even birthday cards—
anything your child wants to keep. He suggests the captions, of course.

Self-Portrait

a life-sized poster

Materials
a large piece of paper
scissors
crayons

Instructions
1. Place a large piece of paper on the floor (several brown paper bags opened and taped together will do). Have your child lie down on the paper.
2. Trace the outline of his body with a crayon.

Activity
Help your child color the portrait. Draw in fingernails, hair, clothes, eyes, ears, nose and mouth. Talk as you work: "What color should the hair be? Is your hair curly or straight? Are your eyes brown or blue?"

When he's finished coloring the portrait, help him cut it out and hang it up for everyone to see.

Variation
Cut out paper or fabric clothes to be tacked or taped on the portrait.

Paper Bag Masks

faces that tell how they feel

Materials
large paper bag
scissors
crayons or felt-tip markers
optional: paper cup, pieces of
   paper, cellophane tape or glue

Instructions
1. Before you begin, have your child put the paper bag over his head. With a crayon, carefully mark where the two eye holes should be.
2. Help your child cut out two holes for eyes.
3. Use crayons to draw the face. If you like, you can use a paper cup attached with cellophane tape for a nose. Paper strips that have been fringed or curled can be glued on for hair.

Activity

Young children have to learn about their feelings and the feelings of others, just as they have to learn about numbers and letters. Since feelings are sometimes hard to pin down, making masks for different feelings will provide a chance to talk about each feeling: "How can you tell if a person is happy?" "How does it feel to be happy?" "How do you act when you're happy?" "What makes you happy?"

Hint: Be ready to accept what your child says. If he says that when he feels angry he feels like hitting someone—accept it. He does. Don't you?

You can help by first acknowledging how he feels: "Yes, you feel like hitting the person who made you angry, don't you?" And then help him think of better ways to express what he's feeling: "How else can you let someone know that you're angry? Yes. You can tell him—and tell him why, so he won't do it again."

181

A Picture Map

of your neighborhood or of your block

Material

a large piece of paper
crayons or felt-tip markers

Activity

Help your child make a *picture map* of your neighborhood. First take a walk to look for things he'll want on his map: the pond, a park, the playground, the vacant lot, the fire-house, Johnny's house, the apple tree and so on.

When you get home, spread the paper on the floor and help your child mark out where each thing will go. Start by marking where you live and the street you live on. Gradually add other streets and places you and your child know.

Label each picture on the map. Hang the map on a wall. Next time you go out, use the map to plan where you'll go before you leave or to show where you've been when you come home.

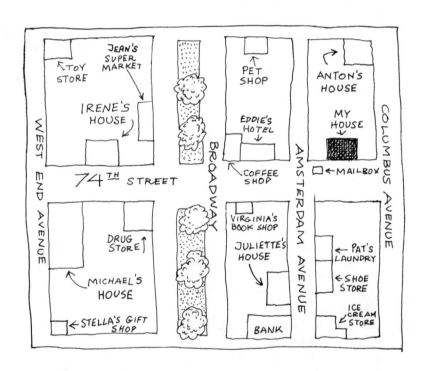

Mail Away

and the fun begins

Receiving mail is a thrill for preschoolers. Take advantage of the coupons you find in magazines, on backs of cereal boxes, under your door or that you receive in the mail. Help your youngster fill in his name and address, stick on the stamp and take the coupons to the mailbox. What excitement when the mail arrives!

A subscription to a magazine is a wonderful gift for a youngster.

Together, decorate a special box for his mail.

183

Play Kits

props for preschool adults

Children love to imitate grownups. And as they do, they learn about roles, jobs and how it feels to be an important person with special tasks to perform. Encourage your youngster to try out new roles and new activities. Your role is to supply the props—he'll do the pretending if you put the right things in his hands. It's a good idea to keep the ingredients for several play kits on hand.

Restaurant Kit

Plastic or paper cups, saucers, plates, tableware, napkins, empty food containers, tablecloth, handmade menus.

Kitchen Kit

Pots, pans, bowls, egg beaters, spoons, measuring cups, measuring spoons, cookie sheets, cake pans. A cardboard carton turned upside down can become a stove.

School Kit

Paper, pencils, crayons, chalk, small blackboard, books.

Supermarket Kit

Toy cash register, play money, price tags, sales slip pad, unopened canned goods, empty food containers, used cake mix boxes, wax fruit.

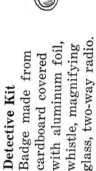

Disguise Kit
An old pair of dark glasses, an old hat, a mustache to cut out, wax false teeth, a false nose, makeup, a wig, a beard.

Post Office Kit
Large index cards, stamp pads, stampers, crayons or pencils, stamps (use Christmas seals), shoe box for each member of the family, with slot cut in front and name clearly printed on.

Cleaning Kit
Several brooms, mops, sponge mops, dust cloths, sponges and paper towels.

Hospital Kit
Adhesive tape, gauze, assorted Band-Aids, stethoscope (a real one only costs a few dollars and your child will be able to really listen to mysterious chest sounds), small plastic bottles, cotton balls.

Detective Kit
Badge made from cardboard covered with aluminum foil, whistle, magnifying glass, two-way radio.

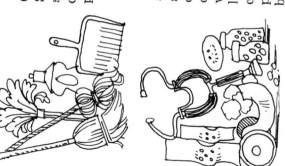

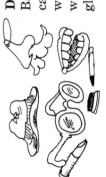

Make a Family Tree

a who's who for your child

Materials
old photographs, paper, crayons or felt-tip markers, scissors, glue

Activity
To help your youngster understand the idea of "family," use old photographs to make a family tree. Make your child the focal point. Help him begin to understand that Uncle Jimmy is your brother. And that Grandmother is your mother. Wherever possible point out shared characteristics—he has the same color eyes as his grandmother. His hair is the same color as his father's and his grandfather's.

Variation
Cut out photographs of family members and let your child use them and/or crayons and paint to make new pictures.

186

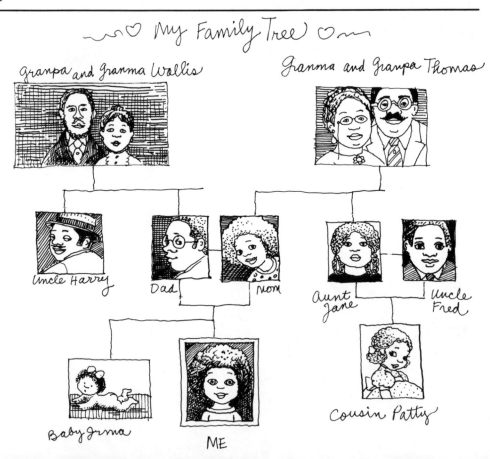

My Family Tree

Granpa and Granma Wallis

Granma and Granpa Thomas

Uncle Harry

Dad

Mom

Aunt Jane

Uncle Fred

Baby Jerma

ME

Cousin Patty

A Special Vest

he can wear and talk about

Materials

vest (if you don't sew, buy one)
felt or iron-on fabric in a variety
of colors

Activity

An ideal present or a joint project
is a vest decorated with things that
are special to your child:

> the family dog
> his goldfish
> a house with your house num-
>   ber
> a bat and ball (if baseball is
>   his favorite game)
> his initials
> your street sign

The decorations can be cut out of
iron-on fabric or cut out of felt and
sewn on. You can also add baseball
team labels, travel labels, and any
other patches that are special for
him.

Blow Up

a picture of him

Surprise your child by having
his photograph blown up into
a life-size poster for his room.
You may want to do the whole
family. Cover a wall with a
collage of posters.

187

Birthday Parties

a special celebration on a special day

Birthdays are important to youngsters. If it's at all possible, plan a birthday party for your child. Don't make it a surprise party. At this age, planning the party is as much fun as the party itself.

Keep the party simple so that your child can help with the preparations. All that's really needed are invitations, a few decorations, refreshments and plans for a game or two that everyone can play when the guests arrive.

DECORATIONS:

Don't spend a lot of money on fancy decorations. Homemade paper chains and party hats are much more fun.

INVITATIONS:

Buy them or help your child make them. Send them out a week in advance. Don't let the party go on too long. Be sure to make it clear on the invitation what time the party is over.

Hint: Enclose a self-addressed stamped postcard that will only require checking and mailing. Each guest can have the fun of answering by himself.

☐ I CAN COME
☐ I CAN'T COME
SIGNED:

Food

The best time for birthday parties is lunchtime. Serve a simple menu plus birthday cake and ice cream.

Hint: Most children would rather eat hot dogs than anything else.

♡ Some Refreshments ♡
You and Your Child Can Make Together

Punch: Use powdered sweet drinks that only need water added, or add special flavors to milk.

Cookies: Make your own by spreading frosting (use home-made or packaged) on graham crackers or vanilla wafers.

Sandwiches: Use cookie cutters to cut out fancy-shaped peanut butter and jelly sandwiches.

Cake: Make cupcakes instead of one big cake. Your child can help with the decorating.

Games

You'll find ideas throughout the book. For example:

Button Toss
Ring Toss
Giant Steps
Bingo
Alphabet Lotto
Questions

A Time Line

putting life in order

Materials
clothesline or string
clothespins
index cards or pieces of paper
crayons or felt-tip markers

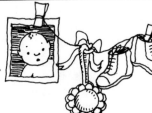

Activity
A time line will help your child get a sense of "where he's at," and where he's going. Help your child pick out the important events of his life:

> the day he was born
> when you moved to where you live now
> when he learned to ride a bicycle
> the day his baby brother was born
> when he went to visit Aunt Mary

Find old photographs or help him draw a picture on an index card or a piece of paper to represent each event. Write the date (or year) of the event on the card. Ask your child to dictate a short caption.

String the clothesline where he can reach it. If you string it along a wall, it won't be in the way. Help him use clothespins to hang the cards along the line in the order they happened. You can vary the spaces between the cards according to the amount of time between the events. Later you may want to add some of the events of your life to the line or make a parallel line he can compare.

Chapter 11
Physical Growth

The difference between an infant in a crib and a six-year-old who can leap in the air, climb down a ladder and pick up a tiny feather on the ground is incredible. As parents look back over the first few years of their child's life, they marvel at the speed with which he learned to crawl, to walk and then to run. "It seems like yesterday he was just a baby." And today? He has developed control over his entire body, his muscles, his nervous system, his bones and his skeleton; he has developed coordination and agility. The result? A child with good health, a sound body and a sense of his own physical power.

Parents can help their children learn to control and enjoy their bodies. They can suggest activities in which the small muscles are strengthened: muscles that help a child draw a circle, pick up a puzzle piece and play finger games. Parents should also encourage large muscle activities that strengthen muscles for running, skipping, jumping, hopping, crawling, pushing, pulling and lifting. They can make sure that their children have facilities outside, either in a backyard, park or schoolyard, for freewheeling, unbounded play.

In addition to muscle development, children should be encouraged to discover how their bodies can be used expressively. How does your body show happiness? What is a "jump for joy"? The plasticity of the body as it assumes different positions can be both serious and funny for children. To this end, a sort of dancelike activity has been included in which children imitate animal movements.

One of the most natural ways to enjoy one's body is through dance. Children know this. They like to learn rhythmic songs, to march to band music and to dance to lively tunes. And since dance, as well as the other games in this chapter, lend themselves easily to group activities, we find that the physical-growth experiences teach cooperation and an appreciation of group fun.

Activity Chart / Physical Growth

Activity	What It Teaches
inside action games	three games: Simon Says, Beach Ball Bounce and Statues
outside action games	three games: Red Light/Green Light, Jump the River and Obstacle Course
animal imitations	using your body creatively to make animal movements
music and dance	enjoying rhythm and body expression, enjoying spontaneous movement
all about muscles	small muscle coordination, large muscle coordination

Inside Action Games

for rainy days

1. Simon Says

The leader gives commands to the players, who must follow every command *except* commands *not* prefaced by the words *Simon says*. Anyone who follows a command that doesn't have the words *Simon says* before it, is out.

2. Beach Ball Bounce

Children enjoy playing "catch" with beach balls, which are bigger and slower moving than the small balls used by their older brothers and sisters. You don't need any particular rules— just play!

① SIMON SAYS TOUCH YOUR HEAD!

② SIMON SAYS TOUCH YOUR NOSE!

③ BEND OVER!

④ YOU'RE OUT!

3. Statues

Find a lively music station on the radio. While the music plays, the children dance or move in any way they please. Every once in a while, quickly turn off the sound. At this point each one must halt and hold, like a statue, the position in which he has stopped. Count slowly to five, then turn up the music for more dancing. If anyone moved while you were counting to five, he is out of the game. (Don't enforce this rule too strictly for very young children.) If you don't have a radio, use a record player or improvise music by clapping your hands or banging a pot with a spoon.

Outside Action Games

who wants to play?

1. Red Light/Green Light

The leader stands at one end of the playground or yard with his back to the rest of the children, who are lined up at the opposite end. When the leader, still with his back to the players, yells, "1–2–3–4—green light!" the players run toward him as fast as they can. When the leader yells, "1–2–3–4—red light!" he quickly turns around to see if all the players have stopped. Any player caught running must go back to the beginning. The first player to reach the leader wins.

2. Jump the River

Place two sticks on the ground about 1 inch apart, thus forming a "river." Each child takes a turn to jump over. Widen the river a few inches and see if the children can still jump across. Continue in this fashion, widening the river until no one can leap over. The last to jump successfully is the winner.

3. Obstacle Course

Set up an obstacle course in your backyard or playground, using cardboard boxes, barrels, milk cartons, ropes, and so forth. Let your child help you decide where the obstacles should go, and what the players must do when they get to them. Jump over? Run around? Crawl under? Once set up, the obstacle course is ready for the children, who try to go through it as fast as possible without upsetting the objects.

Animal Imitations

how many animal movements can you make?

CAN YOU CRAWL LIKE a SNAKE?

CAN YOU FLY LIKE a BIRD?

CAN YOU SWIM LIKE a FISH?

CAN YOU WADDLE LIKE a DUCK?

CAN YOU HOP LIKE a FROG?

CAN YOU GALLOP LIKE a HORSE?

Music and Dance

1. head, shoulders, knees and toes

This activity is a combination exercise game and song, sung to the tune of *There Is a Tavern in the Town*. If you can't sing, chant the verses in a rhythmic manner.

> Head, shoulders, knees and toes,
> Knees and toes
>
> Head, shoulders, knees and toes,
> Knees and toes-s and—
>
> Eyes and ears
> And mouth and nose
>
> Head, shoulders, knees and toes,
> Knees and toes.

(author unknown)

As you name each part of the body, put your hand on the part mentioned. The result is a quickly paced and rather invigorating exercise. Maybe you can get the whole family to do it once a day. Make up additional verses by naming different parts of the body: heels and nose, neck and waist.

"HEADS...
SHOULDERS...
KNEES...
TOES..."

2. rhythm band marches

Improvise instruments from the kitchen:

> bang a large pot with a spoon (drum)
> jingle two spoons together   (castanets)
> crash two pot lids together   (cymbals)
> bang two wooden spoons together (rhthym sticks)
> shake a ring of measuring spoons   (tambourine)

Show the children how different sounds are made by different materials and different sizes of instruments.

3. spontaneous dancing

Give your children plenty of opportunity for dancing, the most expressive way to develop coordination and rhythm. Put on a record or turn on the radio and dance away!

All About Muscles

small muscles

Hand and finger coordination is important. Help your child learn to:

lace his shoes
button buttons
open and close snaps
color with crayons

cut paper with blunt-edge
  scissors
pick up small objects, such as
  puzzle pieces

large muscles

Nurture a strong healthy body by giving your child plenty of opportunity to:

walk   leap   skip   push   stretch
run   hop   jump   pull   dance

Index

72 73 74 75 10 9 8 7 6 5 4 3 2 1